·LETTER·
CARVING

ANDREW J. HIBBERD

·LETTER· CARVING

TECHNIQUES & PROJECTS TO HONE YOUR SKILLS

THE GUILD OF MASTER CRAFTSMAN
PUBLICATIONS

First published 2015 by
Guild of Master Craftsman Publications Ltd
Castle Place, 166 High Street, Lewes,
East Sussex BN7 1XU

All photographs by Andrew J. Hibberd except for the following pages:
5, 10, 11, 12, 13, 58, 118, 119, 126, 127, 134, 135, 142, 143, 150,
151, 162, 163, 170, 171, 178, 179, 192

ISBN 978 1 86108 952 6

A catalogue record for this book is available from the British Library.

Publisher Jonathan Bailey
Production Manager Jim Bulley
Senior Project Editor Sara Harper
Editor Jane Roe
Managing Art Editor Gilda Pacitti
Designer Chloë Alexander
Additional photography Anthony Bailey and Mark Baker

Set in ITC Berkeley Oldstyle BT, Interstate and Charlemagne
Colour origination by GMC Reprographics
Printed and bound in China

CONTENTS

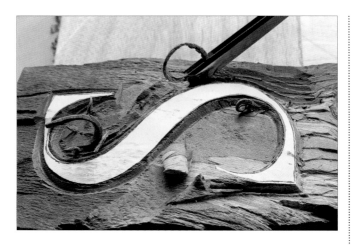

TECHNIQUES & PRACTICAL EXERCISES

PROJECTS

INTRODUCTION

I HAVE WRITTEN this book after spending many years working in the fascinating and absorbing but often frustrating area of letter carving. You may have little experience of the craft, or maybe you are at a more intermediate level of skill, or perhaps you have been carving for years but have developed a desire to tackle letter carving. This book has been produced to direct and support you in your quest to learn more.

The book is technique based, starting with a series of practical exercises. It is structured in such a way as to encourage you to tackle more interesting and complicated letter-carving projects in what I hope is a seamless progression, and to achieve ever higher standards of craftsmanship. It also aims to steer you through the difficult periods that often occur when learning a new skill.

I am aware that we carvers can at times be an impatient bunch. A newly acquired clean piece of oak or fruit wood, slate or limestone is just too tempting a target to resist with our freshly sharpened chisels. Please trust me, though, when I say that the more preparatory work and practice you do, the clearer your understanding, the faster your progression and the more satisfying the results will be.

It is very easy to believe that a well-considered design, an understanding of letterforms and accomplished letter-carving techniques are skills that only those who carve stone possess.

Although wood is rightly perceived to have certain technical difficulties associated with the grain of the material, this is by no means a restriction on the formation of beautiful calligraphic lettering. While I was training at the City & Guilds of London Art School, it was the norm for woodcarvers and stone carvers to work alongside each other in the life drawing and modelling studios. Although at that time I was not trained in the art of letter construction, I am sure that the processes of drawing, design, pen and brushwork were conducted by both sets of students together.

Over the last seven or eight years in the 'lettering world' I have seen many wonderful examples of perfectly executed and brilliantly designed wood- and stone-carved lettering commissions. Both wood and stone projects are included here for you to try.

I am passionate about this art form in all its various guises. Many years ago I was advised by a valued friend and mentor never to let a piece of work leave your workshop unless it is the best you are able to achieve at that time. This has been repeated to me many times over the years, by many people. If there is an ethos behind this book it must be that with the will to succeed, the right tools for the designated material and a well-understood design, anything is possible.

And don't forget the enjoyment part!

Fine-tuning the lettering before the final cutover

THE HISTORY OF LETTERING

IN THE early 20th century, the Swiss linguist Ferdinand de Saussure suggested that language is the 'glue' that joins abstract concepts such as thoughts, emotions and perceptions with sound. When repeated, taught and used among people, it encouraged collective ideas to emerge. In the ancient world such ideas had to be shared face to face and by word of mouth, so they were restricted by virtue of being so localised. Everything changed with the advent of early descriptive codes such as hieroglyphs and Cuneiform; for the first time, information and ideas were recordable and transportable. Centuries later, when scholars deciphered these language codes using such artefacts as the Rosetta Stone (Egypt, 196 BCE) (**1**) these language-recording devices not only transcended space but also time.

EARLY FORMS OF WRITING

Phonetic alphabets started to appear around 6000 BCE. However, it was when the Sumerians developed a form of writing known as Cuneiform (meaning wedge-shaped in Latin) in around 4000 BCE that methods of communication began to speed up. A wet clay tablet was used as a kind of notepad to record wedge-shaped impressions formed by a stylus or tool. Many examples can still be seen in museums today, providing scholars with a wealth of priceless information. Presumably designed as throwaway objects, ironically they have turned out to be extremely durable (**2**). Cuneiform in its many guises spread throughout Mesopotamia and survived until its decline from 539 BCE with the rise of the Persian Empire. It briefly reappeared again between the 3rd and 1st century BCE.

This now brings us onto the Phoenicians, an ancient people located in the eastern Mediterranean. Theirs was a highly skilled technical civilisation, but for us their main claim to fame

The Rosetta Stone: unlocking the language of the past

Clay tablet inscription in the style of Akkadian cuneiform (860 BCE), produced from a drawing of a stone-carved object in the Ashmolean Museum, Oxford

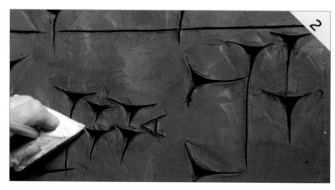

was the development of a standardised phonetic alphabet, the forerunner to our Roman alphabet. The Phoenician civilisation spread across the eastern Mediterranean, founding colonies and over time exploring most of the then-known world. In the 6th century BCE Phoenicia became part of the Persian Empire but with the rise of Greek power its days were numbered.

CURSIVE WRITING: SCRIPT, JOINED-UP WRITING OR HANDWRITING

I will now examine the diverging pathways between epigraphy, the art of writing on a durable material, and the newly developing 'cursive' handwriting, quick and not necessarily expected to last. Working with wood and stone is time-consuming and costly, making these materials unsuitable for use on a daily basis. It was now possible, however, using Cuneiform and the developing alphabets, to record information in a quick and easy fashion. Precursors to paints and inks were developed and the suitability of other writing surfaces such as broken pot shards was explored. Information exchange and record-keeping were now readily available to the masses. Everything from household accounts, business deals and lawmaking could be accurately recorded and many example still survive today. These examples have given historians and philosophers valuable insights into the everyday lives and experiences of these people.

PARCHMENT AND VELLUM

The earliest example of writing on animal skin dates from ancient Egypt nearly 5,000 years ago. The material used to write on was parchment, produced using the skin of animals such as goats and sheep, and vellum, a finer parchment usually made from calfskin. The skins were treated in an identical manner being limed, scraped and dried under tension, but vellum was more expensive, as it was a finer quality material. Both were extremely popular materials to use in the medieval period, when superb handwritten and handcrafted books were produced. Works of art as well as fonts of wisdom, these books would often take years to complete. They were written in monasteries by monks trained as scribes.

Page from the Luttrell Psalter, one of the most important medieval manuscripts

SCRIBES

In ancient Egypt scribes were powerful individuals, often holding great sway at court. Formally educated in hieroglyphic script writing, the records they produced formed the basis of our knowledge of ancient Egypt. Everything from storytelling to economic activity was recorded and scribes consorted with other professionals such as painters and artisans and, presumably, carvers. They controlled other workers and craftsmen, overseeing the construction of monumental and important buildings. Scribes in medieval Europe were equally skilled but did not hold such an exalted position in society.

Ancient Egyptian sculpture of a seated scribe (2620–2500 BCE)

PAPER

In 105 CE, a Chinese court official called Ts'ai Lun was credited with the invention of the papermaking process, albeit not quite in the form we know it. Paper had been available for a couple of hundred years before this ancient entrepreneur set the wheels in motion for its production, but it did not, however, catch on straight away. Japan acquired it in around 600 CE, Egypt in the 10th century and Italy in the 12th century. Although it was widely used in the Middle East, Europe was slow to embrace paper. This was partly due to religious reservations about accepting technology from the Islamic world, and also for commercial reasons. There would be a huge loss of trade in animal products such as vellum and parchment if this usurper paper took over. Everything of course changed with the development of printing technology and the publication of the Gutenberg Bible in the 15th century. Everything was now in place to allow the masses to have access to books.

EPIGRAPHY

In Italy, with Greek influence, the production of inscriptions and memorials started to spread throughout the Etruscan civilisation. In about 600 CE, skills learnt by Etruscan craftsmen led to the development of the Latin alphabet which consisted of 23 letters. Our modern alphabet is, of course, based on the Roman alphabet with the addition of the three letters J, U and W in Medieval times.

Roman capital inscriptions proliferated throughout the empire, the most famous of which is Trajan's Column, erected in 113 CE in honour of Emperor Trajan's victory in the Dacian Wars. Unfortunately in 1897 the column was 'cleaned up' using acid, presumably applied with wire or scrubbing brushes. This process surely destroyed some evidence of how the letters were produced. The Romans left no manuals explaining their letter carving techniques, so we can only wonder how much technical information has been lost forever.

LETTER CARVERS

It is difficult to pick apart the working practices and lifestyles of the wood and stone carvers of the past, who created such exquisite letter carving work. Even naming these people can be problematic since a lot of work was not signed. I am convinced, however, that Edward Catich, in his book *The Origin of the Serif*, is correct in his view that the formation of letters by Roman and probably Greek craftsmen is directly attributable to brushes being used on stone rather than pens or reeds. These brushstrokes, he suggests, were added either directly or indirectly onto the material to be carved. From a completely practical point of view, a brush works better on a rough textured surface than a reed or a pen. It was one of the techniques I used in my training and is an important part of the ethos of this book.

An example of Roman letter cutting

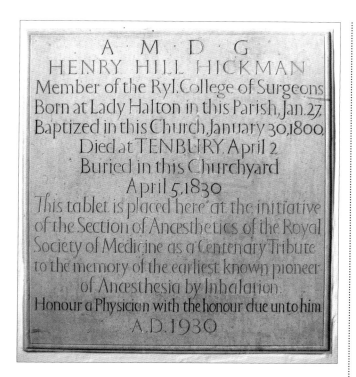

A memorial stone in Bromfield Church, Shropshire. Designed by Eric Gill and cut by his assistant Lawrence Cribb, 1930

In 1928, Gill set up a lettering workshop, Pigotts, at Speen, Buckinghamshire. Among the apprentices he trained were brothers Joseph and Lawrence Cribb and David Kindersley. Kindersley set up his own workshop in Cambridge in 1945 and became a major force in lettering design, producing – like Gill – his own fonts and a large volume of important work. He too trained a number of important exponents of lettering and letter carving including his own son Richard, Kevin Cribb (Lawrence Cribb's son) and David Holgate.

LETTER CARVING TODAY

Historically, formal lettering such as majuscule (upper case) letters tended to be used in monuments and inscriptions. However, from the Modernist Revival begun by Eric Gill to the present day, letter cutters have had no such restrictions. Calligraphic lettering fonts using informal hand are now used. Minuscule or lower case letters; italics, slanted or upright, in upper or lower case, are all now part of ever-more sophisticated designs in both wood and stone carving commissions.

Letter carving today is in many ways similar to how it was in times past. Many stone memorials and plaques are still hand-drawn and hand-carved, and destined to reside in our grandest cathedrals and the humblest of churchyards. Artistic lettering works abound in both wood and stone, often with a modern contemporary feel about them. These can end up as part of a sculpture trail, in a gallery or museum, or just in someone's garden. House signs and house numbers are still very popular as commissions, again carved in either wood or stone, with or without additional decoration. Modern technology has also entered the picture, and sophisticated designs can be produced using power tools controlled by digital design equipment. But will this ever replace the human carver? I hope not.

Perhaps scribes were employed as and when required to draw or paint letters onto stone or wood. These letters could then be modified if required during the carving process by the letter cutter. After all, if scribes collaborated with other tradesmen and artisans when producing their own work, why not return the favour if costs permitted? Extending this line of reasoning, perhaps there were lettering craftsmen with both sets of skills available; scribe and carver. This would negate the need to employ someone else, would probably be cheaper if quality were not compromised and would also speed things along.

MODERNIST LETTER CARVING

Moving forward several centuries, under the tutelage of Edward Johnston, Eric Gill revitalised letter carving in what Philip Burgoyne (1955) describes as the Modernist Revival. Johnston's book, *Writing & Illuminating & Lettering*, published in 1906, describes how Roman capital letters, if written quickly in everyday script, gradually changed over time to develop into a kind of shorthand, the development of the cursive hand. Somewhere along the line, lettering as a means of communication and lettering as an art form began to diverge. In the time of the Luttrell Psalter, they were of equal presence. Now, in our craft, the art form predominates while the communication function has diminished.

LETTER STRUCTURE & CARVING METHODS

THE PREVIOUS section briefly described how letterforms developed and were used over time. Here we look at the structure of the letters themselves, to define the parts of letters and the terms used in letter carving today, and to introduce the carving methods used in the exercises in this book. You may find it helpful to refer to these pages when you start drawing letters and practising carving.

TYPES OF WRITING

There are three types of writing: formal, semiformal and informal. A letter can be broken down into its component parts. As long as each one of these is produced in one action this constitutes writing. Formal lettering tends to have the most components, for example, the letter 'R' can have three, four and possibly five strokes. The same letter, using informal writing, uses only one stroke, with the writing implement never leaving the paper.

Formal lettering tends to be slow and meticulous, the letters being separate with no ligatures. Semiformal is quicker; the letters are often compressed strokes which may be extended to become ascenders and descenders. Informal lettering is casual and workaday, using a pen, pencil or chalk.

LETTER STRUCTURE

The following terms shown on the diagrams are used as standard by letter carvers. The only 'rule' I use is to carve from 'thin to thick'. The bar of a capital 'A', for example, will always be my starting point on that particular letter. The other important issue I take note of, in both wood and stone, is the vulnerability of certain sections during and after the carving process. The apex of the capital 'A' and the junctions on the letters 'W' and 'V' are good examples of this.

The thought processes on the flexible approach I take when deciding the sequence of cuts needed to carve a letter have been formed by the following considerations:

- A large variety of tools are used when carving 'V' cut letters in wood, as opposed to the one or two used when carving letters in stone.

- We all vary in height and flexibility, perhaps have certain physical challenges, or are maybe naturally left-handed. No one size fits all in the carving process, so the drawings in this section are for general guidance only, showing the way that I approach the carving of these particular letters, nothing more.

The arrows show the direction of strokes when using a brush. This sequence of steps is almost the opposite of what I would use during the carving process.

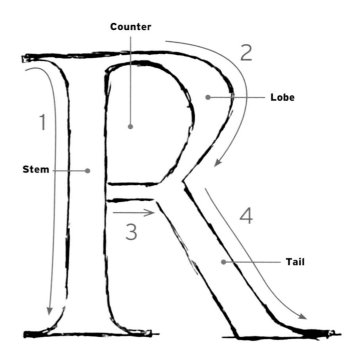

Capital letters (majuscules)
The illustrations show a series of capital letters in which the order of cuts is marked out in red.

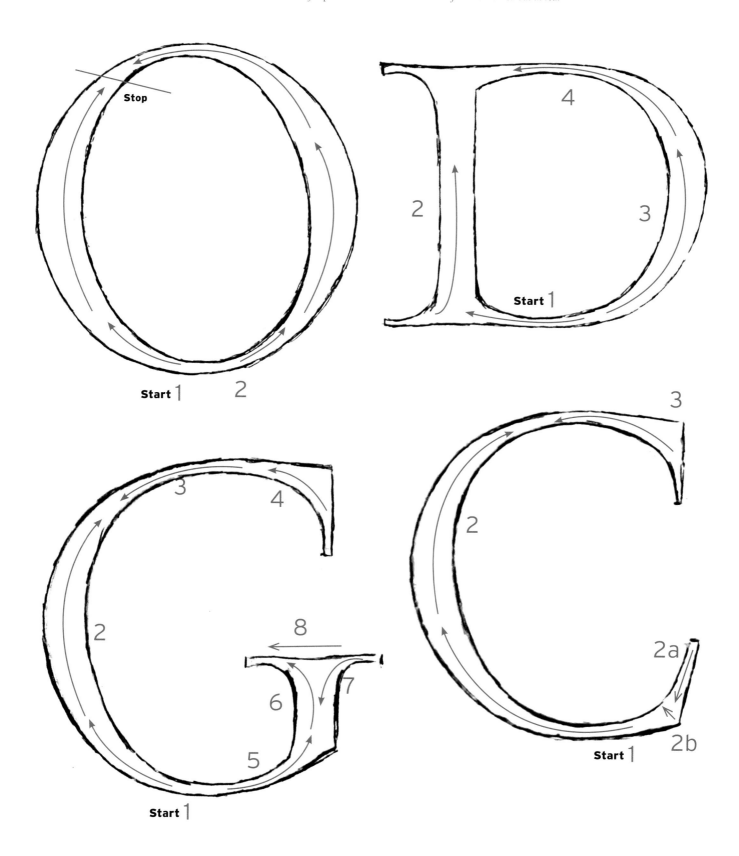

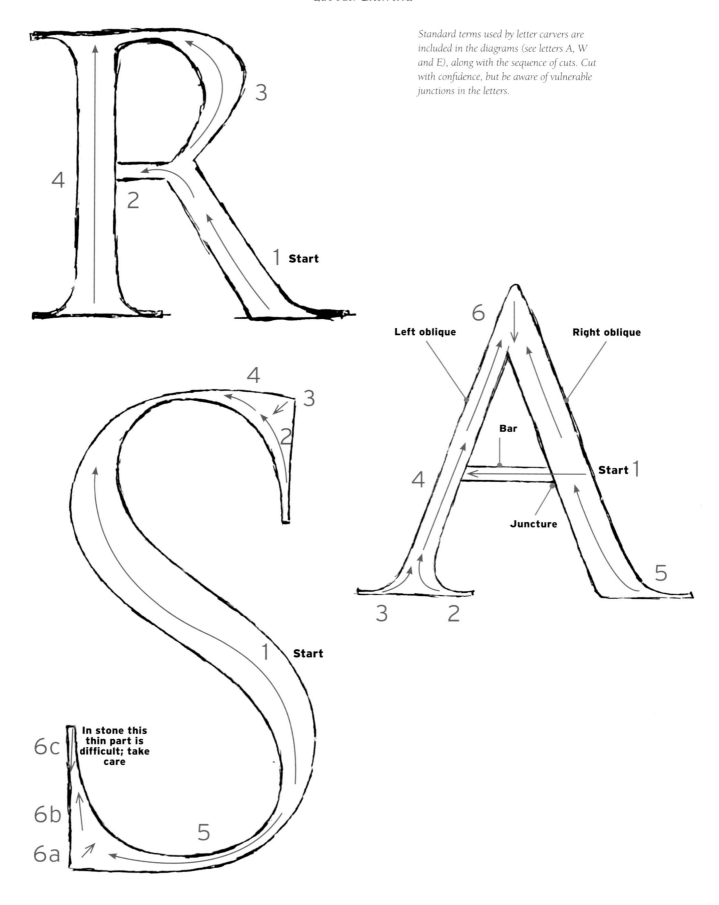

Standard terms used by letter carvers are included in the diagrams (see letters A, W and E), along with the sequence of cuts. Cut with confidence, but be aware of vulnerable junctions in the letters.

Left oblique

Right oblique

Bar

Start 1

Juncture

6

4

5

3   2

In stone this thin part is difficult; take care

6c

6b

6a

1   Start

4

3   2

1   Start

4

5

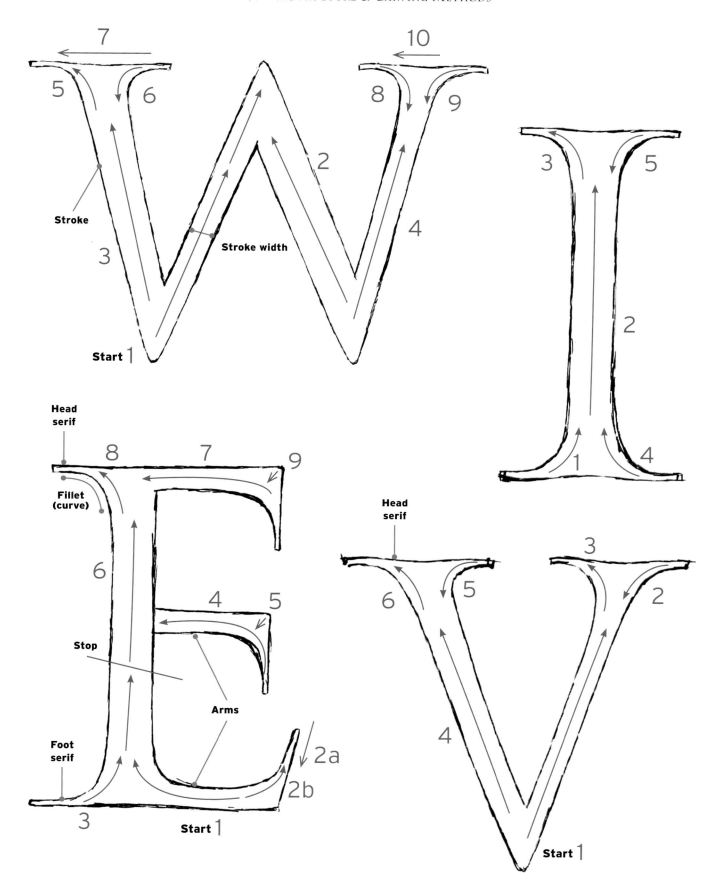

7

10

5

6

2

Stroke

4

8

9

3

Stroke width

Start 1

3

5

2

1

4

Head
serif

8

7

9

Fillet
(curve)

6

Head
serif

3

4

5

Stop

6

5

Arms

4

Foot
serif

2a

3

Start 1

2b

Start 1

Lower case letters (minuscules)
The ascender is the part of the letter that extends above the 'x' height top line; the descender extends below the baseline. The x height is the height of a lower case letter without ascenders or descenders, and the fraction shows the proportion of ascender/descender to the x height that is required for a well-balanced letterform. The cant refers to the angle at which the brush is held.

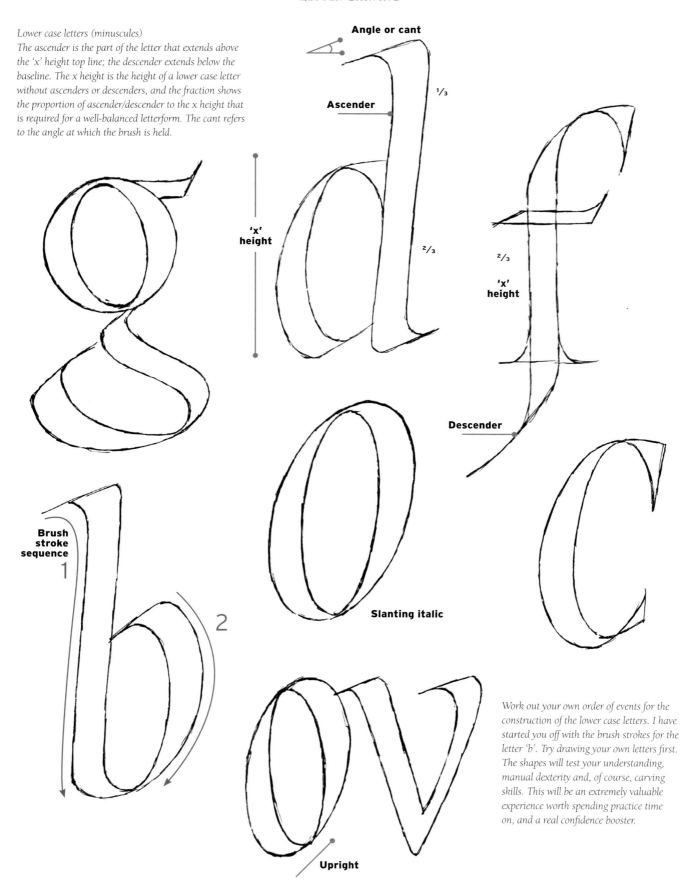

Angle or cant

Ascender

'x' height

$^1/_3$

$^2/_3$

$^2/_3$

'x' height

Descender

Brush stroke sequence

1

2

Slanting italic

Upright

Work out your own order of events for the construction of the lower case letters. I have started you off with the brush strokes for the letter 'b'. Try drawing your own letters first. The shapes will test your understanding, manual dexterity and, of course, carving skills. This will be an extremely valuable experience worth spending practice time on, and a real confidence booster.

CARVING METHODS

Projects in the book are executed in wood and stone using the traditional method of translating a two-dimensional line drawing, brushstroke or pen stroke into a three-dimensional carved design. A carved letter is the result of the removal of a letter shape, or the removal of background material surrounding the letter shape, thus allowing you to be able to read the letter. Within this book the basic methods of letter carving are as follows: incised, when material is removed from within the structure of the letter and raised, with letters that are produced when the background material is removed.

'V' CUT INCISED LETTERING

As its name suggests, this type of lettering has an inverted triangular cross-section, which can vary in depth when the angle at the junction of the two strokes is altered. In a 'V' cut carved letter, the stone dust or wood shavings on the floor are the actual letter being removed, the space left behind is what you see. The letter carver and sculptor, David Holgate, mentioned this several years ago and I have never forgotten it.

Carving using this type of lettering produces two side walls meeting at the centre and base of a symmetrical 'V' cut. This is my preferred method, particularly when carving wood. By changing the angle of the 'V' cut, thus altering the depth of the cut, the visual effect of the carving can easily be altered. Changes in the shadows produced can be emotionally very powerful, altering the mood of the piece. Flat-bottomed incised letters are, in my opinion, far too time-consuming to be produced only using hand tools such as chisels. If technology is involved, of course, they are far easier to produce.

Raised lettering on the Mock Tudor gable of a building in Southwold

FONTS

There are thousands of fonts to choose from, hundreds of which I'm sure are suitable to use in carving scenarios. For the projects in this book, I have selected a couple of favourites to keep things simple: Patten Wilson, and Gothic Black letter. The rest of the lettering is devised from my own training, experience and drawings.

SQUARE-CUT INCISED LETTERING

I have only used projects in wood with this type of lettering because of the vulnerability of the square edges in stone. To speed things up I used a router in conjunction with chisels and gouges. In the right situation and, depending upon the design, they can be very effective, producing dark shadow. I particularly like them in Gothic script (see the Gothic letters 'A and K' produced using a router on page 102).

RAISED LETTERING

Designed and drawn by hand in this book, this type of letter carving is inevitably 'sans serif' (without serifs – those small, decorative flourishes at the end of strokes). Even if you were able to carve them, a small piece of unsupported wood suspended in mid-air would not remain intact for long. Background material is removed with a router, leaving the letters standing proud. The newly formed letters are normally encapsulated within a panel of some description to afford some protection from breakage. I save raised lettering projects for stone or when using power tools such as routers on wood.

The sans serif letters are enclosed in a surrounding panel for protection

·THE BASICS·

*This section focuses on the tools and equipment you will
need to create the projects and exercises in this book.
The machinery used to process the timber and stone is not
discussed here as the materials I used were sourced fully
prepared to my specifications from trusted workshops.
Certain powered technology such as the bandsaw and router
allow me to arrive at the pleasurable side of hand working
by removing some of the mundane drudgery involved in the
earlier stages of the process. If a piece of equipment, powered
or otherwise, is the right tool for the right job, then I will use it.*

TOOLS & EQUIPMENT

HAND TOOLS can generally be thought of as extensions of our bodies, allowing us to manipulate and change materials. They can be placed in general categories and may involve activities such as chopping, cutting, banging, clamping, drilling, marking and holding. Tools and equipment can be used on their own or together in varying combinations, such as mallet and chisel, pencil and ruler.

WOODCARVING TOOLS

Woodcarving chisels and gouges are numbered according to their sweep (the curvature of their cutting edge) and width in millimetres. There are two numbering systems generally in use: the Swiss and the Sheffield. All the examples in this book have been made using Pfeil (Swiss-made) tools, but you can use whichever tools you prefer. See pages 26–9 for a full list of tools and shapes. The tools I use are listed in the box below. Please note that those prefixed with a 'D' are a medium-sized version, suitable for those with small hands and also ideal for beginners because they are easier to handle. Tools prefixed with an 'S' have a skewed edge, and those with an 'F' have a fishtail, useful for fine-tuning those hard-to-reach areas.

> **TOOLS I USED**
> Firmer: D1/8
> 'V' parting tools: D12/2, 12/8, 12/10
> Flat skew chisels: D1S/12, D1S/8
> Gouges: D5/12, D5/8, D8/4, D8/10, D9/2, 3/22, 5F/8
> Veiner: D11/1
> Large 'off the flat', No. 1, 25mm dia.
> Small carpenter's chisel, 5mm wide
> Small forward bent tools
> Dummy/mallet roughly 1lb (460g) in weight

CHISELS AND GOUGES

There is a huge variety in the range of chisels and gouges available for woodcarving; less so in stone. Chisels and gouges are designed to cut specific shapes to a particular depth in a designated material; for our purposes either wood or stone. How successful they are depends on several criteria: the design, shape and quality of the tool, combined with the skill of the person using it, this last being the most important.

Sheffield	Swiss
No. 1	No. 1
No. 2	No. 1S
No. 3	No. 2
No. 4	No. 3 – almost identical to Sheffield No. 4
	No. 4 – halfway between the Sheffield No. 4 and No. 5
No. 5	No. 5 – almost identical to Sheffield
No. 6	No. 6 – fractionally less curved than the Sheffield No. 6
No. 7	No. 7 – halfway between the Sheffield No. 6 and No. 7
No. 8	No. 8 – fractionally less curved than the Sheffield No. 8
No. 9	No. 9
No. 10	There is no equivalent to the Sheffield No. 10 in the Swiss range to date
No. 11	No. 11 – far more acute ellipse around its cutting edge than the Sheffield No. 11
No. 39	No. 12

MALLET

The mallet allows you to exert sufficient force upon a sharpened tool to cut your chosen material accurately and consistently over a period of time. If you're trying to cut delicate letters in oak or a similar hardwood, a lightweight woodcarver's mallet or stone carver's dummy is all you need; tougher material may require a heavier mallet or a more energetic approach. There are many variables to consider – too many to cover here – but the most important consideration is control. The mallet must be comfortable in your hand, and it shouldn't even come close to the maximum weight you can handle. You want it to become an unnoticed extension of your hands, even after a long session at the bench. A correctly weighted mallet is therefore very important.

BUYING TOOLS

If you are relatively inexperienced at carving or have decided to upgrade or change the tools you generally use, a period of familiarisation – handling – is important. Before purchasing any expensive tools, I suggest asking your woodcarving club (if you are a member) or a woodcarving friend if they will allow you to test some of their chisels. At the very least, visit the tool supplier to handle the particular gouges you wish to purchase before you buy. Buying an unknown or unfamiliar tool online is probably not a good idea, unless they will accept its return with no questions asked.

When purchasing a new carving chisel or gouge (a general rule of thumb: gouges are curved and chisels tend to be flat) I consider a few simple but very important factors: does it look pleasing, is it nicely designed, well made and elegant? Does it immediately feel comfortable in your hands? Is the steel thick and unwieldy, needing a regrind and sharpen before it can be used effectively? Once in use does it hold an edge, or, frustratingly, are you constantly having to sharpen or hone it back into effective use? When carving for long periods does it continue to be comfortable to use? Of course you won't know the answer to the last two questions until you've actually bought the tool, but your experience will help you with future purchases. Finally, does the manufacturer or supplier offer a suitable range of tools to enable you to extend your repertoire with the advent of new projects?

A comprehensive set of woodcarver's tools with the addition of the 17/6, a useful intermediate size tool

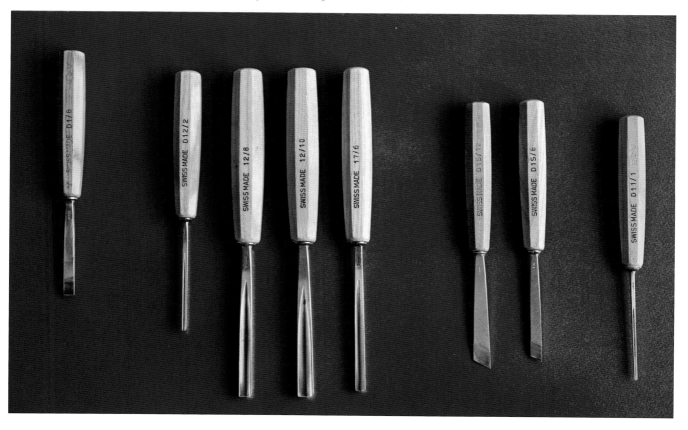

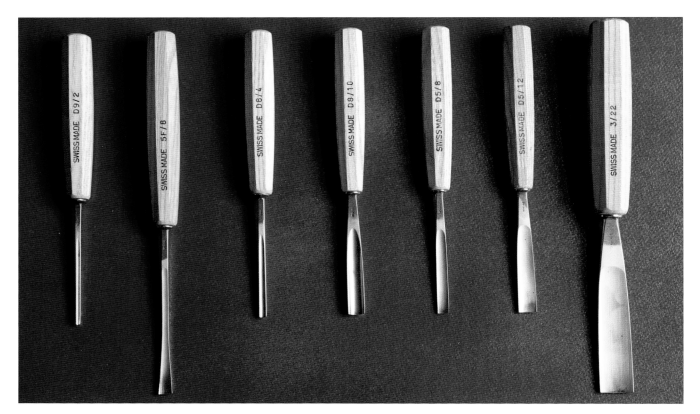

A comprehensive set of gouges

My favourite second-hand chisels and stone carver's dummy

Second-hand tools, of which I have many, generally perform brilliantly – the steel has hardened over time and takes a fine edge, and they also tend to be thinner with a large variety of shapes and sizes. Well used, comfortable and loved, they have stood the test of time, except of course if you're unlucky! The rust which you thought was superficial might be deeply ingrained – it won't hold an edge as the steel needs re-tempering – the first tap with a mallet and the handle splits or falls off! There is always risk attached to buying tools in this way, but it is one I have always tended to take.

Types of chisel vary in design depending upon the job they have been designed for. A mortise chisel is strong and wedge-shaped to enable it to chop into a piece of wood. If you are tempted to use a carving chisel in the same manner, expect a shattered and broken tool.

Carpenter's chisels can be used for certain tasks in the carving process; the Bench project on pages 170–77 is a case in point. As a general rule, however, I would not consider using them as the only tools in most carving projects. Trying to sustain an uncomfortable grip on the shoulders and ferrule of these particular tools for several minutes, let alone several hours, is not recommended.

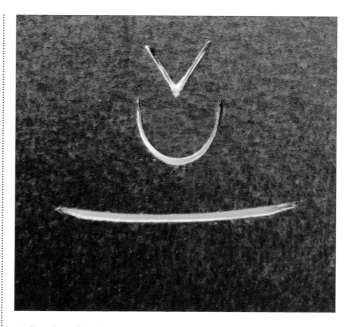

Profiles of an off the flat number 1, through to a Scoopy number 11, with a 'V' tool thrown in for good measure

When used correctly and highly sharpened, the edge of a chisel exerts a huge force as it cuts into the surface of the timber. It will provide a clean-cut, perfect finish to the wood surface, unsurpassed by other finishing methods.

A boxwood handled carpenter's gouge (below), next to an elegant modern carving tool (top)

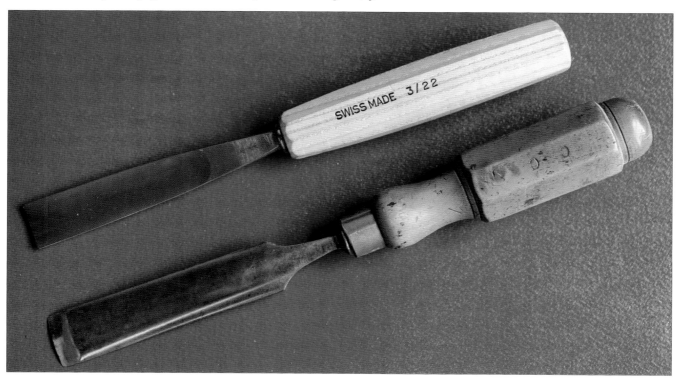

CARVING TOOL SHAPES AND PROFILES according to the Sheffield list

NUMBER   **PROFILE OF CUTTING EDGE**

Straight tools	Long-bent tools	Short-bent tools	Back-bent tools	2 ¹/₁₆	3 ¹/₈	5 ³/₁₆	6 ¹/₄	8 ⁵/₁₆	10 ³/₈	11 ⁷/₁₆	13 ¹/₂	14 ⁹/₁₆	16 ⁵/₈	20 ³/₄	22 ⁷/₈
1	-	21	-												
2	-	22 23	-												
3	12	24	33												
4	13	25	34												
5	14	26	35												
6	15	27	36												
7	16	28	37												
8	17	29	38												
9	18	30	-												
10	19	31	-												
11	20	32	-												
39	40	43	-												
41	42	44	-												
45	46	-	-												

The Sheffield numbering system, as discussed on page 22, showing the curvature or shape of the sweeps (cutting edges) from No. 1 to No. 46.

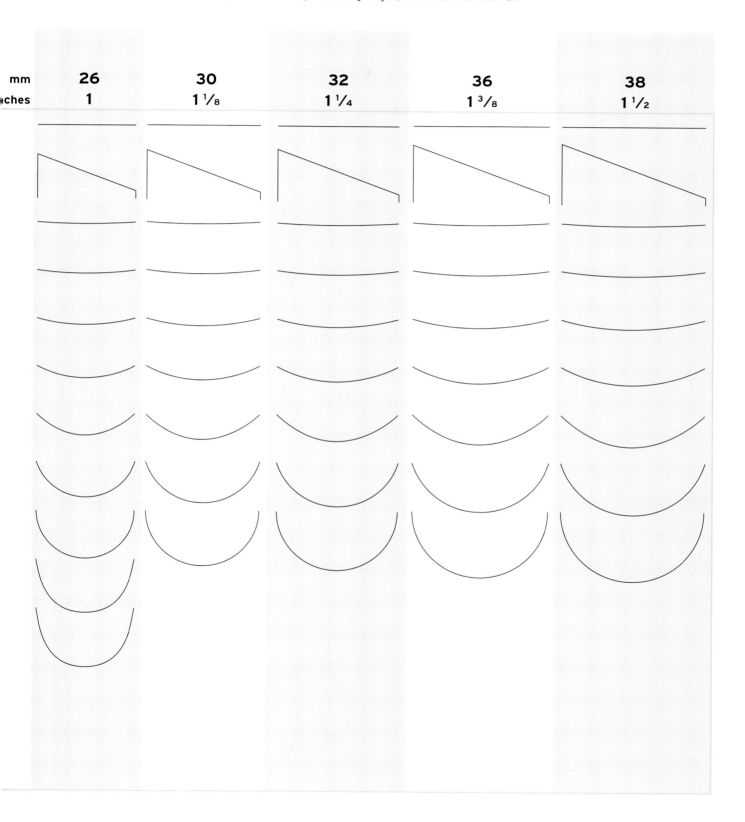

CARVING TOOL SHAPES AND PROFILES according to the Swiss list

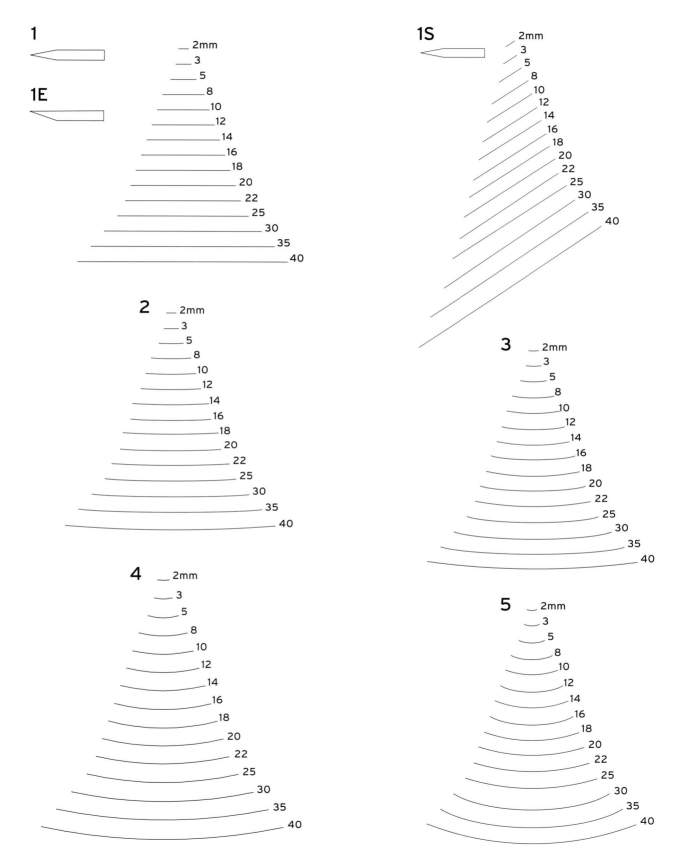

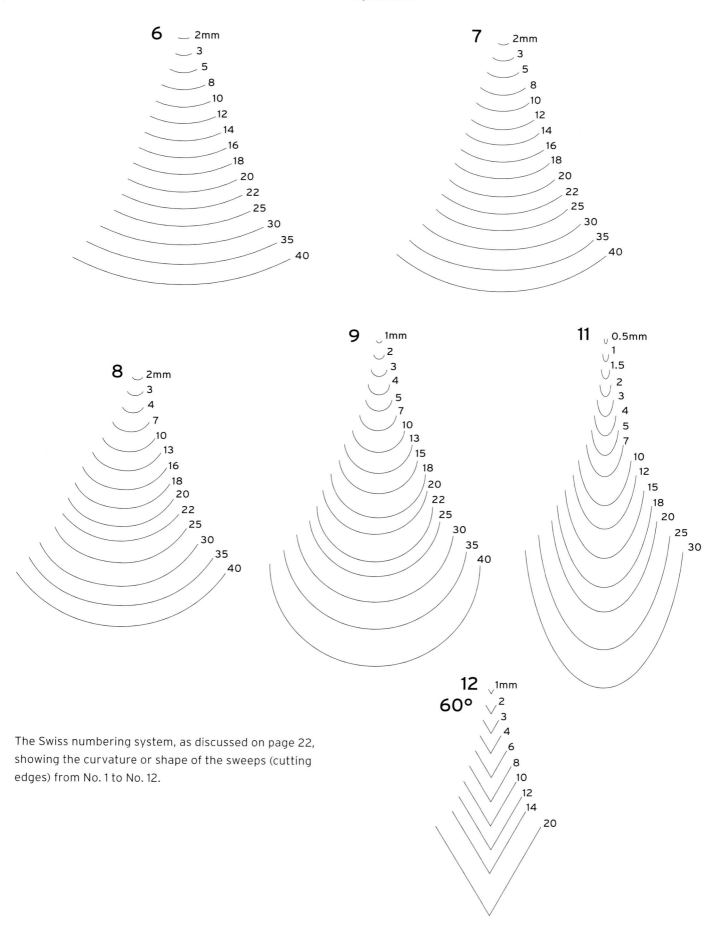

The Swiss numbering system, as discussed on page 22, showing the curvature or shape of the sweeps (cutting edges) from No. 1 to No. 12.

The stone carving tools selected for the projects in this book: lettering chisels (3mm, 6mm and 10mm), bouchard or bush hammer, claw, stone carver's dummy

STONE CARVING TOOLS

You will only need three chisels for the projects in this book, all of which are modern and tungsten carbide tipped. The body of the tool is constantly being struck by one type of mallet or dummy; it therefore needs to be softer than the tungsten carbide tip to nullify any shattering impact damage.

The other tools shown are a claw and a bouchard or bush hammer. These are used to remove and shape stone, as demonstrated in the Grapes project on pages 142–9. If the tool marks are left they can also add texture and body to a design. On occasion this can happen by serendipity, but do not leave it to chance too often!

The wedge of tungsten carbide can be seen clearly

A homemade general woodworking bench

THE WORK AREA AND CLAMPING METHODS

The working area contains many benches and jigs. The choices you make will be based on your budget, whether you have the time to make any equipment, and also whether what you make or can buy will be robust and professional enough for the job. Other issues to consider include working height, movability around a fixed point, and portability. There are plenty of professionally made carving stands and benches available to buy. I own several and use these in conjunction with my own jigs designed to hold and support work, taking health and safety issues into consideration at all times.

My multi-sloped bench with the detachable wooden top in place. You can make something similar to suit your own particular requirements – see picture, right

MULTI-SLOPED BENCH TOP

I have devised a multi-sloped, portable bench top which can be clamped or screwed to a workbench or table. It has two detachable wooden boards, one of which has a built-in window to act as a light box. Another that can be used as a support for the purposes of drawing/painting and carving. There is a shelf at the back for resting tools and equipment on, with a storage compartment underneath. At the front you can rest tools and paintbrushes while working, or place a low-wattage light into position when the light window is used.

Drawing of my portable multi-sloped bench, with a light window in position

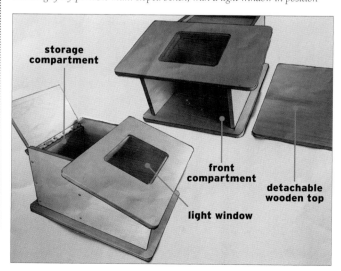

storage compartment

front compartment

detachable wooden top

light window

My vertical carving stand

VERTICAL CARVING STAND

This is a homemade device that I use for demonstration purposes because it is portable and can be taken apart and quickly reassembled. The basic structure is made using sturdy scrap wood. There are two triangular side sections which are joined together by two crosspieces of wood clamped into position using four hardwood wedges. The size and types of material that you use in your carving will dictate the type of additional structures you need to add to something like this. For example, I have added a centre section using two large square section posts to which I have added wooden cross section pieces. I am now able to either screw or clamp pieces of wood to this, which I will then carve. In the case of stone I can rest small pieces of slate on the sections and then add further restraints to stop them falling off. This is just to give you an idea of how you might tackle some of the problems of supporting your work during the carving processes.

When positioning a large stand such as this you need to consider its footprint in conjunction with the amount of space surrounding it. This is where you will be working and tight, cramped conditions can lead to mistakes and even injuries. Large pieces of work need to be carefully fitted or placed on a bench or stand, because constantly moving large pieces of wood or stone is not really an option. You may need to manipulate the environment to suit the working conditions, such as adding additional lighting.

HOLDING WORK

Attaching wood or stone to benches and stands is always a matter of good judgement, with safety being paramount. Methods of attachment for wood include paper joints and screws (where they cannot be seen). Leaving areas of waste wood on a blank allows for ease of attachment by either clamps or screws. These can be removed later when the carving is complete. Stone is generally supported upright on the stand with additional restraints to stop it falling forwards.

The jig used for the Norney wood project

A simple sharpening system consisting of two diamond strips attached to a piece of hardwood, carborundum stones, slipstones and a leather strop

SHARPENING SYSTEMS

I have tried many different arrangements over the years, which have included using grinding and honing wheels plus a plethora of sharpening stones, new and second-hand. You probably have your own methods and ideas relating to sharpening, so I will just briefly touch upon a few. Grinding machines can be purchased with interchangeable parts that include wheels of differing abrading qualities. They often also include attachments for honing and buffing, used as part of the finishing process. Nowadays, when needed, I tend to only use slowly revolving grinding wheels with a water tray attachment. High-speed grinders may be prone to overheating and bluing of the metal, and there are numerous health and safety considerations to take into account. You must wear eye protection and gloves because of the danger of flying debris and sparks, and you may need to wear a mask because of the possibility of metal dust. Digging in with the tool while the wheel is revolving at high speed can be dangerous.

A mechanical grinding machine

The simple sharpening method I currently favour is the one profiled in this book (see pages 74–7). It consists of two diamond strips attached to a piece of hardwood for serious grinding, and a couple of medium grade carborundum stones, one of which is shaped, for the next stage, then fine Arkansas slipstones of varying shapes to complete the sharpening process. Pieces of leather with a honing compound applied are then used as strops. For very small tools, I often just use metal polish in the groove produced by that particular tool.

Some of the basic equipment required for drawing and painting

DRAWING AND PAINTING

I have used quite a lot of different materials for both the techniques and the projects in this book, but you may well not have the budget or the inclination to buy the same. Please check the equipment lists on the relevant pages because you may be able to borrow equipment or use particular items for multiple purposes. At the very least, however, you will need a high quality chisel-ended paintbrush, watercolour paints, dip pens and water-based inks; pencils, charcoal, a graphite stick and white chalk; graph paper with cm squares for scale drawings, and good quality drawing and tracing paper for designs. Instead of tracing paper I use C300 detail paper, which is a translucent paper similar to tracing paper but much more economical to use, because it comes in rolls and you can cut off the amount required rather than using pre-cut sheets.

A plunge router with an attachment jig

POWER TOOLS

Small hand-held plunge routers (6 or 13mm/¼ or ½in) are exceedingly useful devices for removing background material, particularly in raised lettering. Routers basically act in two ways: firstly, the straight down plunge action, which almost replicates drilling a hole. The pitfalls to this technique are that, if you come into contact with a knot or changing grain, it can throw you off to one side. If you plunge too deeply and too quickly, burning and smoke will ensue, which doesn't suit either the machine or the blackened timber. Secondly, having set and locked in the depth of the cut, the router can be manoeuvred to cut a channel or groove into the surface of the timber. With practice and using a variety of cutters, accurate shapes working to quite a fine line can be cut out. When used in lettering both 'V' cut and flat-bottomed cutting is

Tungsten carbide-tipped router bits

achievable. Again there are pitfalls, particularly when working close to design lines. Occasional snatching can occur which can easily cause you to cut through a section that you are planning to keep. Likewise, if you start trying to remove too much timber, as was previously explained, more stress will be applied to the router motor and more smoke and blackening will occur.

Always follow the manufacturer's advice regarding the use of the machine, work well within its limitations and comply with all its safety features.

MARKING TOOLS

I have used a hard 6H pencil for tracing purposes and drawing on stone. In all other applications a softer HB pencil was used. On dark stone I used white chalk crayons or pencils because lead pencil marks would not have been visible.

Several right-angled squares were used in the drawing and woodwork stages of the projects, including tri-squares both large and small, set at 90° and 45°. Two pencil-marking gauges were used to run parallel lines on both wood and stone. I also used metal rulers of varying lengths, a set of compasses, measuring callipers and plastic curves.

A selection of tools that are used for marking, clamping, levelling, measuring, attaching, resizing and squaring up

TIMBER

THE WOOD types used in this book are oak (*Quercus robur*), beech (*Fagus sylvatica*), pine (*Pinus spp.*) and tulipwood (*Dalbergia decipularis*). Other timbers I have used in past lettering projects have included lime (*Tilia x europaea*), pear (*Pyrus communis*) and apple (*Malus domestica*). You may have had success with other varieties local to you. Wood is infinitely variable and enormous changes in grain texture and colour can occur within one tree. When you extend this out and start comparing different species, sourcing your wood can seem rather daunting. The wood chosen for the techniques section was of poor quality, only being fit for purpose as a practice piece cut with razor-sharp chisels.

The right tools for the right job?

A FEW THINGS TO LOOK OUT FOR WHEN EXAMINING A PLANK:

- Are you actually able to recognise different types of wood in plank form? This is not as easy as it sounds; never be embarrassed to seek advice.
- First impressions are important – does it fit within your design concepts, is it workable using the tools you have at your disposal?
- Expect some minor splits or shakes but do you foresee a problem now, or expect further problems to ensue?
- Are there signs of twisting, cupping or warping? Check the end grain: was it cut flat or quarter sawn? Will it continue to move while being worked? At the very least ask plenty of questions. If unsure about its quality, reject it.
- Does the grain change direction, possibly causing problems when carving?
- Is it naturally seasoned or kiln dried?
- Does it look properly seasoned and stable and have a moisture content suitable for your needs? If it is too dry, it may crack or split.
- Is it worm free?
- Timber with densely packed fibres, such as boxwood (*Buxus sempervirens*) and some of the fruit woods, are well suited for letter carving.

Note the distinctive annual rings on this piece of scrap pine

ANATOMY OF A TREE

This is a chainsaw cut section of a relatively quick-growing tree, a conifer of some description I believe. The annual rings number around 20 and it was cut in around 2013. Even without a dendrochronologist's knowledge we can start to make sense of elements within the structure of a tree.

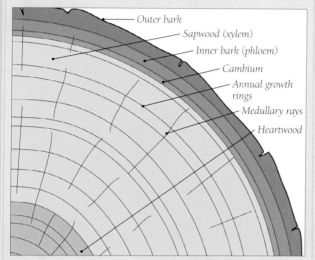

- Outer bark
- Sapwood (xylem)
- Inner bark (phloem)
- Cambium
- Annual growth rings
- Medullary rays
- Heartwood

This cross-section of a tree imparts valuable information

The annotated picture below shows how the wood moves when cut in particular ways. Quarter sawn is always cited as the most stable and produces beautiful figuring patterns in timbers such as oak. It is also probably the most expensive, so you will need to factor that into your costings when sourcing timber.

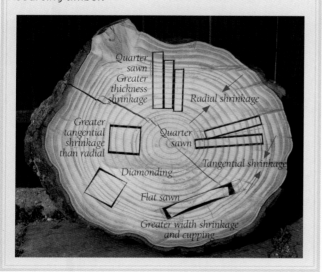

Quarter sawn
Greater thickness shrinkage
Radial shrinkage
Greater tangential shrinkage than radial
Quarter sawn
Diamonding
Tangential shrinkage
Flat sawn
Greater width shrinkage and cupping

CHOOSING YOUR TIMBER

If you are a green woodworker then you will already have your own sources of material and the means of processing them. If, however, like me you have neither the time, capacity nor equipment to process timber from the tree stage then you will have to rely on the expertise of others to source your timber. Starting with word-of-mouth and a little bit of research should generally throw up a plethora of interesting and hopefully knowledgeable people to help.

Having chosen your local saw mill or timber supplier I would suggest a personal visit to explain your requirements while hopefully establishing a productive relationship. Always keep a record of these visits noting all the pointers and tips you glean, thus you start building a portfolio of useful knowledge. Where possible try to acquire sample pieces of interesting wood for practising on. I often add notes to these samples to keep for future reference.

KNOTS AND BRANCHES

When a tree develops a branch it causes disruptions to the annual rings. Severed branches or knots are a natural part of timber, their twists, turns and colour variations can also enhance the appearance of the wood. Inevitably they affect the grain of the timber, often in drastic ways, so learning to handle this anomaly while carving is a pretty important skill.

A large bough in a mature tree exerts forces upon the trunk of the tree. The extension strength and the compression strength of the timber above and below the branch can result in differences within the plank.

Notice the vessels, part of the sap transportation system

WOOD IDENTIFICATION

VESSELS OR PORES

In the picture above you can see the annual growth rings, and vessels or pores in the inner bark. These serve as a series of pipelines used by the live tree for sap transportation and are one of many methods used in tree identification. They are only found in hardwood; softwoods use tracheids for their sap movement. The end grain photograph (below) gives a clearer idea of the structure of this particular section of an oak tree.

Hardwoods tend to be divided into three main categories when making reference to the vessels: ring porous, semi ring porous and diffuse porous. Because of the huge diversity of timber species around the world, this is another means of narrowing

A lovely piece of oak showing its distinctive end grain

COMPRESSION DAMAGE

The yew *(Taxus baccata)* wood used to construct bows was cut deliberately to take advantage of the compression strength. For us, however, compression damage accidentally done when applying undue pressure onto the timber using a tool or clamps is not so beneficial. Sometimes you can raise the grain to remove this by ironing with a damp cloth over the damaged timber. This will raise the nap of the grain of the timber and improve the situation. Equally, spilling water onto a finely carved or sanded finish has an adverse effect on that finish requiring more work.

---

down the choices when seeking identification. Whole articles relating to the differing arrangements of these pores have been written; it can become very technical very quickly!

RAYS

Another useful cell type to help with identification are rays. Found in most tree species, they are used for the movement of nutrients within the living tree. Angled at 90° to the rest of the fibres, they can be seen clearly in the end grain. They too are as diverse as the trees they are contained within and as technical a subject as the vessels.

While many other methods of tree identification are used, for our purposes distinguishing between the timbers used in this book is easy as they all look radically different from each other and fulfil the purpose required of them.

SOURCING PRE-DIMENSIONED BLANKS AND TIMBER BOARDS

Sourcing the correct timber for the correct job needs to refined when dealing with specific projects. For example, where food is involved, particular types of timber such as beech are used due to their inert nature and the fact that they will not contaminate the food. A wavy edged plank, possibly with the bark still in place, may be a design consideration. The finish of the timber on occasion needs to be of a very high standard, and as knot-free as possible. If you have specific dimensional requirements, it can be exceedingly frustrating if the timber that you have ordered needs to be recut or even reordered if unsatisfactory. This delays the work, and in a professional environment could incur costs. It all goes back to whether you are able to source reliable suppliers for your timber requirements.

WORKING WITH THE TIMBER

As carvers we are always looking to make life easier for ourselves so working with the timber is clearly preferable to having to fight the material. You often hear terms such as 'working with the grain' mentioned when referring to carving but it is only when you carve yourself that you realise the significance of this term. Again to try and keep things simple I have photographed a few randomly picked samples of wood from the woodpile alongside the professionally machined oak used in the Oak Lodge (see pages 118–23) and Anno Domini (see pages 126–33) projects. These photographs highlight some of the differences in the way grain looks and changes.

This is a piece of clean oak ideally suited for our lettering purposes (**1**). Notice the rays and the vessels, and, importantly,

Beech blanks

Pear wood blanks

how the fibres curl around the small knot. This photograph (**2**) shows a piece of the vulnerable edge broken off but more importantly highlights the fibres, part of the structural nature of the tree.

An ideal piece of oak, a blank canvas for your lettering

One of a multitude of fibres structuring the tree and a nasty splinter!

Splitting wood in this way (**3**) can quickly remove material, and by not forcing it into a certain pathway, produces a better result. An industrial saw cuts through a log and everything in its path with no regard to the grain movements and natural split of the tree. Riven planks, cut by hand, are more flexible and stable, but also of course prohibitively expensive. The natural finish on this piece of spalted beech clearly highlights the differences over this technique and a piece of sawn wood (**4**). It also shows how the very lively grain would visually detract from fine letter carving. Providing of course you were able to cut said lettering in such constantly moving and undulating grain. Possibly from the same beech tree, this piece of riven wood clearly shows the rays (**5**). It has split very easily and accurately, having no knots to cause problems. Unfortunately, it has suffered due to water ingress and the rotting process. This piece of timber shows a large angle of shift by the grain (**6**) – imagine trying to carve this if it were planked! I suspect you would be cutting into the grain from whichever angle you approached it from.

Splitting timber, working with the wood

A beautiful design created in decline and death

Another design, with almost a digital feel

A sculptural effect with spiralling twists

TIMBER TREATMENT, FINISHING AND CONSERVATION

We can resist the attacks and slow down the rate at which timber deteriorates often by very simple means. If you place completed work or seasoning wood directly in contact with the earth, thus adding water to the equation, observe what happens: staining, rot and an open invitation of fine dining for the local wildlife! (**7**), (**8**), (**9**), (**10**), (**11**). A simple solution is to remove this contact when installing the wood and establish a surrounding air flow.

The regular application of paint, varnish or oil can slow the onset of deterioration, although eventually over time even this ceases to be a viable option (**12**).

If general maintenance is in place, the properties of the materials themselves help slow down the destructive processes. Oak, for instance, hardens over time, resists pests and ends up a pleasing silvery grey colour. Structural beams in old properties at first glance appear to be wormy and rotten, however, generally once you are through the surface layer the wood inside is as hard as iron.

No longer fit for our purposes but still a habitat for a plethora of species

An old piece of timber clearly showing tangential and radial shakes

A large section of apple wood completely rotten and gradually disappearing

The only part of this elm post to survive was above the ground

This log now provides a habitat for a diverse mix of flora and fauna

Even though positioned onto a stone base and protected with paint, major repairs are required

STONE

THE IDEAL stone to use for the projects in this book are Caen stone, Portland limestone and slate. I have not used either sandstone or granite, as you need specialist tools and professional experience before attempting to work with these materials. The properties we are looking for in stone suitable for us as carvers to use are similar to the properties required by our other favoured material, wood, namely: longevity, hardness and consistency.

Quietly crumbling away

The surface has flaked off

Ideally the stone should have a clean surface that is mostly unaffected by anomalies and with no large colour changes. The texture of the stone needs to be consistent; not too soft or crumbly, or equally too hard or difficult to work. Anything that may detract from seeing the shadows of the carved letterforms, particularly when carving fine delicate lettering, should be avoided if possible.

WEATHERING

Stone, like wood, can suffer decay; certain limestones and sandstones can weather rather badly. You can often see in churchyards memorials where the lettering has disappeared altogether due to the top surface flaking off. The three main causes of this damage are salt crystallisation (the worst), acidic attack caused by air pollutants and frost action (**1**), (**2**), (**3**).

SALT CRYSTALLISATION
Porous stone absorbs a mixture of salt and water either by capillary action or from access via the cracks and fissures of the stone. When evaporation occurs the salt is left either

Signs of powder on the brickwork below

Serious deterioration and blistering

Deterioration and the presence of moss

Note the staining of the stone

The damage caused by a dripping pipe

within the structure or on the surface of the stone, or both. The surface salt layer is called fluorescence and the salt crystals within the stone structure are called crypto fluorescence. Over time with constant wetting and evaporation this intrusive salt forms pressure, which can affect the integral structure of the stone. Crumbling occurs and powder forms, often followed by structural failure of some description (**4**), (**5**), (**6**).

ACIDIC POLLUTION

Industrial processes produce pollution, some of which contains sulphur-based particles. When mixed with water these particles can produce sulphurous acid, which in turn can have a serious effect on limestone and marble buildings, either causing the stone to dissolve or a black crust of gypsum to form that undermines the stone's stability.

FROST ACTION

Large sections of stone can flake off due to the pressure caused by the contraction and expansion of water turning to ice. There will be no powder produced or blistering of the stone, which is associated with the damage caused by salt infiltration. Proper building maintenance and repair and choice of stone not so susceptible to this type of problem can help to alleviate matters (**7**).

A stockpile of collected stone weathering outside

Try cutting a few test letters where they won't cause problems, then store this stone outside subject to the elements for a period of time (**8**). This may help you determine its suitability for the purpose you require.

Try to identify stone used historically for letter carving within your local area. Has it weathered well or particularly badly? I then suggest you try and source the successful stone, if it's still available, of course! Skilled architects and stonemasons in the past didn't always get it right, and were (obviously) unaware of our particular industrial pollutant issues. So seek out advice and purchase the best stone you can find for your particular purpose from quarries or stone yards.

If carefully positioned outside, your stone carving will settle into the environment and hopefully survive until the next millennium (**9**). If you reside in a more temperate climate you may not experience these type of deterioration problems, and may use different types of locally sourced stone.

SOURCING THE STONE

Stone can be sourced directly from the quarry, or from stone yards. Transporting large pieces of stone is an expensive business and returning them to be replaced by another piece of stone is doubly expensive. You need to be sure the stone you have ordered is suitable for the purpose you have in mind. If you are able, visiting a stone yard and buying offcuts is always a good idea. Often you can form a relationship with the staff there and they will set aside for you suitable pieces of stone that would otherwise have been scrapped.

Garden centres often have small boulder-shaped pieces of stone useful for practising on; you may even find the odd gem among them. If there are any professional stone carvers in your area, have a chat with them. In my experience they are very open and friendly people and can provide you with some useful contacts.

One of my first stone carvings on top of a piece of oak, both weathering nicely

TYPES OF STONE

Below are brief descriptions of the main types of stone suitable for letter carving. The materials available will of course depend on where you live but specialist suppliers can help you to decide what might be suitable for your purposes.

LIMESTONE
Portland South coast of England: suitable for carving lettering
Caen stone French: a medium stone and good to carve
Lepine French: creamy, a bit softer than Caen
Clipsham North of England: good for carving and for producing bold letters
Ancaster North of England: several grades of hardness

SLATE
Welsh slate in particular has always been prized for detailed carving but slate is sourced from all over the world: Australia, America, Turkey and India, for example. The thing you really have to determine, though, is how it will weather outside in your particular climate. Could it become structurally compromised in wetter, colder conditions where ice could cause de-lamination in certain types of slate? Those with texture, consistent colour and which are made up of dense material that weathers well, are ideal for letter carving.

Riven slate Can provide an interesting texture but can be difficult to letter carve.

Fine rubbed slate Perfect for detailed letter carving. 'Rubbed' is a term used to grade the mechanical finish produced at the stone yard; you can consult with them as to the type of finish you require, e.g. matt to highly polished.

STONE PREPARATION

Stone has a form of grain, particularly the sedimentary rocks, such as limestone, which were built up in layers, known as the bed. This has to be taken into consideration when carving. Sculptures are generally not carved with the block standing upright and the bed at right angles to the ground. The stone will weather better when in the correct orientation. Slate that has been split or cut parallel to the bed will work well and be of uniform colour. If it is cut at an angle to the bed, it will cause the slate to vary in colour. In extreme circumstances, if it were cut across the end grain it would be almost impossible to carve.

I will not go into any great detail about stone preparation, or the use of the point, the claw, chisels and other associated banker mason tools. For practice pieces, use offcuts of prepared stone. For particular projects, I suggest you purchase the stone already prepared. Stone yards have the correct machinery to do the job: stone preparation and banker masonry skills are a whole new area of expertise, far outside the remit of this particular book.

HEALTH & SAFETY

The author with a good supply of safety equipment

I KNOW IT is tempting to overlook this section and skip through to something more interesting, but if I can hold your attention for a few minutes, it will be useful to discuss some health and safety issues without getting too technical or bound up with rules and regulations. Before using any piece of mechanical equipment, think through what the risks are both to yourself and to others. Do not rush the job; this is where mistakes can happen and problems can occur. Remember that if you do have time constraints, injuring yourself is certainly more time-consuming than taking a few minutes of extra care! I always try to think my way through each project before I begin work. This has many benefits: it focuses your attention on the job in hand at the start of the process and will re-engage you if you are returning to the project after a break. These can often be pivotal moments, costly in time if you get it wrong! I hope the information here will start a train of thought within you and will help you to work safely and prevent a future injury.

Equipment needed during the routing process

ESSENTIAL SAFETY EQUIPMENT FOR YOUR WORKSHOP

- Dust mask or a dust extraction system. Consider working outside if the working environment is especially harmful.
- Safety glasses or an all-over head mask.
- Ear defenders.
- Foot protection, such as boots with steel toe caps or, in exceptional cases, shoes with chemical-resistant soles.
- Gloves. Different varieties are available, ranging from very fine medical ones to thick leather gauntlets.
- Thermal underclothes and socks and an overall if you will be working outside in the cold for a long time.

RISK ASSESSMENT AND SAFETY CONSIDERATIONS

- Always read through the manufacturer's instructions before operating machinery.
- Survey the work area for trip hazards and badly stacked timber and equipment.
- Store sharp chisels and gouges safely. Brushing against a badly positioned chisel can result in a painful cut.
- Tidy the workspace between each project. As well as giving you a well-deserved break, it also allows you to set up the space in a manner suitable for the next project.
- Tie back long hair and/or loose clothing that could become caught in the machinery.
- Check that your carving is secured correctly.
- Adjust the working height so that it is comfortable and correct for you. This will help prevent back problems.
- Make a realistic assessment before lifting a piece of stone or wood. Generally it is not the large piece of stone that you know is impossible to move that is the issue. The real problem is the smaller piece of stone that you mistakenly feel you can lift.
- Do not allow children or animals in your workshop.
- Attend a course on the safe usage of power tools.
- If you are demonstrating or working alongside other people, consider taking out public liability insurance against accident or injury. This does not negate the need for good safe working practice, but it can offer you some peace of mind.

Removing unwanted dust without having to remove your dust mask

Choosing the right block to lift may not be as straightforward as you think

LIGHTING

T HE LIGHT reflecting off a micron's thick chisel edge is known as the candle. It tells us that additional sharpening is required before a perfectly carved finish can be achieved. The same light – while casting shadow – picks up shapes formed during the carving process when the letter is being steadily revealed. Light is obviously a major factor in our work allowing it to shine, both physically and metaphorically. The combination of light and shadow gives the work depth. Light, however, can also magnify the slightest error or blemish. There is nowhere to hide other than to seek perfection in every aspect of your work.

Light and shadow reveal texture and sharp edges

THREE-DIMENSIONAL WORK

Light has always been an important element in both art and sculpture as it allows us to have three-dimensional awareness. The pen, paintbrush or pencil can be used during the design stage to give an interpretation of a carved letter. The reality, though, is that a painted letter or any added mark on a page is still only two-dimensional. To produce three-dimensional carving a change of plane is needed, light is required and material has to go!

My setup for using artificial light

Natural light produces a well lit letter

Reverse the shadow for a different perspective

THE WORKING SETUP

Natural sidelight is my preferred method of illuminating the work environment. Using a portable stand allows for orientation into the best possible lighting position for all carving applications. On gloomy days or when working in the evenings, artificial light is required. I use two powerful lights on portable stands, with a small portable light adjacent to the carving stand to fine-tune the lighting environment.

LIGHTING THE WORK

Having mentioned the positive factors of light there are also negative ones. Poorly lit work can produce misleading shadows that may affect the quality of your carving. An example of this in a 'V' cut letter is the misinterpretation of the angle of slope on one of the two sides. This could cause a mismatch in your carving angles, which, if not spotted early, may become a problem. To counteract this, I make one side slightly more illuminated than the other, using either natural or artificial light. You then end up with two contrasting shadows thus allowing you to interpret the 'V' cut shape accurately (**1**). To reverse the shadows, hold your hand up in front of the more powerful of the two lit surfaces. Even with less light there is still enough of a contrast between the two shadows to enable you to spot any anomalies that were hidden before (**2**). It also gives you a different visual perspective on the carving, particularly the top surface edge, which should not be overlooked but sometimes can be.

The edge of the letter may be full of wobbles and inaccuracies, the pencil line may even have been accidentally removed. With poor lighting, these problems may not be noticed until it is too late. The only recourse then is either a design change or the use of sandpaper to bring matters back on track.

The junction of the 'V' cut, the deepest point, needs to be seen and not overcast by a misleading shadow or shadows. If it is overcast, you could incorrectly relocate the baseline, thus causing further problems. Often a simple readjustment of the lighting system, or a slight movement of the carving stand is all that is needed.

Problems can also be caused when poorly lit work hides detail and does not reveal enough information about the carving material during the carving process. When the wood or stone are correctly lit, all blemishes and flaws are revealed. Even minute scratch marks caused by a tiny burr left on the chisel edge can be seen on the slightly polished surface of a newly cut piece of timber.

The shadow is starting to creep up the opposing slope wall

As the sun moves around, it creeps further up

Direct sunlight washes out the carved letter

Simple 'V' cut chisel marks are revealed by light

LIGHTING A FINISHED PIECE

The lettering on a completed piece of work located outside, such as a house sign or a memorial, will often change appearance during the day. This can be due in part to the movement of the sun casting shadows (**1**), (**2**). Adverse weather conditions such as rain can wash out the visual effect of carved letters on stone. Sunlight shining directly onto a piece of wood can appear to fade the letters (**3**) and clouds can cast shadows that obliterate lettering detail (**4**), (**5**). Obviously the weather is outside your control, but sometimes a little thought before installing a piece and then a few simple adjustments may help matters somewhat. Testing the location for light conditions with a sample piece of carving before installation is a good idea. Other means of projecting carved lettering in difficult lighting situations have been tried in the projects and further practice in this book; see for example the gilded 'A' (pages 110–15) and the standing stone (see pages 162–9).

In shadow, the marks fade away

PAINTED LETTERS

Painting carved letters has always been one solution for lighting issues. Gilding can elevate lettering and was popular in the past before electric light was available. Candlelight is captured in a beautifully opulent way by this form of decoration, which is probably why in certain time periods it was so heavily used (**6**).

Candlelight is beautifully reflected by the gilded letters

·TECHNIQUES·
& PRACTICAL
EXERCISES

Having created or modified your own working environment,
and sourced suitable tools and equipment, it is now time to start work.
This stage is all about trying out techniques to help you become familiar
with letter construction and carving and increasing your skills
and confidence with further practice. For me, a clean piece of paper and
a brush filled with paint producing the first letter strokes is as pleasing
as the first chisel cuts on a wood or stone lettering project.

PROJECT DESIGN & DEVELOPMENT

T HIS IS a particularly difficult section to discuss because there are no hard and fast rules as to what constitutes good design. A lot of the time it is simply a matter of taste and this varies with different people. Why is one piece of lettering a beautiful work of art, while another is not? What comprises 'correct' lettering? Copperplate lettering can take your breath away, but why?

A letter constructed using a pen or a brush can have symmetry, flow and artistry. Well-considered negative space (the space that surrounds an object or an image) plays its part in producing forms that are pleasing to the eye. Lettering can be instantly recognisable and epitomise a period in history such as Gothic (medieval), Art Nouveau and Art Deco.

INSPIRATION

Thumbing through old lettering and calligraphy books often leads to ideas and inspiration; the lettering in the Norney wood project (see page 178) was found this way. Start by collecting your own source file with cuttings from magazines, old books and photographs.

Inspiration can come from many sources; as well as a visual stimulus it can come from the buzz you get when discussing things with a kindred spirit. Seek out ideas from fellow carvers and artists, and visit galleries, museums and historic buildings.

The author at home, lost in thought and seeking inspiration

When you are seeking inspiration, ideas often come at the most inopportune time. Keep a notebook by your bedside so you can write down ideas whenever they strike. It's a good idea to carry a small sketchbook and camera around with you. I recently spent a day seeking inspiration for lettering designs in my home city of Norwich, which led to me taking an eclectic but exciting mix of photographs, some of which are shown here. Start exploring your own environment for inspiration: who knows what you may discover? Try drawing any interesting lettering you see around you. This is a good way to improve your technical skills and will also help you to find 'the essence' of the lettering. Make notes on your drawings and look for similarities in letters. Be aware of the negative space and look for the overall 'flow' of the letters. As in nature, there should be no jarring odd angled lines or strokes, unless of course it is your intention to unsettle and possibly to surprise your audience.

A flagpole, part of the Lutyens war memorial in Norwich, unveiled in 1928 but moved to its present site in the Memorial Gardens in 1938 for the City Hall inauguration

An old fire point sign

Details of the flagpole (above and below)

Curvilinear letterforms, characteristic of Art Nouveau-style lettering

David Holgate's plaque celebrating the architect of the Royal Arcade, Norwich

Lutyens' war memorial, Norwich, 1928

Notice the angle of the 'O'

Detail of the font

Carved lettering has a longevity that allows important messages and thoughts to survive for generations. Equally the letters themselves can often be of their time and resonate with us on different levels. The Art Nouveau period (1890s–1914) in particular is one of my favourites, being instantly recognisable with its undulating, organic letterforms. David Holgate's beautifully constructed and elegant script carved on a circular plaque triggers memories for me of many happy hours spent drawing letters under his tutelage and friendship.

17th-century graffiti scratched on the walls of Norwich Cathedral

BEGINNING A DESIGN

The first step is to jot down notes and sketch some rough ideas. Sometimes just playing around with a doodle can develop into something more substantial; this was how the block print project came about (see pages 150–61). Using a brush to sketch out your ideas can help transfer your mood or feelings into the fluid strokes it produces.

After the initial sketches, you should make a scale drawing. Calculate the size of the design, working out the letter spacing and the stroke widths. Think about the type of shaped blank that will be required and how this will affect the perspective. Decide on the positioning and layout and whether you will use raised or incised lettering. Start sketching a design and then produce a scaled-down drawing. Any size and spacing issue can be thought through and adjusted at this early stage. At this scale it is also easier to see everything.

As a general rule a capital letter such as 'A' should just break out of the topline of the 'x' height (see page 18), otherwise it will appear to be too small. A letter such as the 'T' just wants to tip down lower, to be just under it.

When checking a line of lettering for each individual word I tend to look at them in blocks of three. Take the word 'italic' and break it down into 'ita' 'tal' 'ali' and 'lic'. Ask yourself the question: is the letter in the middle of the group closer to either one or other of the outside letters? If the answer is yes then move it slightly closer to the other letter, in a more central position. It's as simple as that, really!

If you are spacing a word within a block of wood or stone, the section below it should be slightly bigger than the section above. Equally the space on the left end should be slightly larger than the space on the right. In the word 'italic', the ascenders and the dots of the 'ls' would mean a very slight adjustment upwards for this word.

You can use a piece of cardboard for checking angles and stroke widths. Look at the 'T'. Mark a couple of pencil lines showing its dimensions. This is the smallest width for this type of stroke. Next take measurements for the widest stroke. With these three pencil lines on the piece of card go around all of the letters and adjust the stroke width to conform to these marks, using your best judgement.

Lightly laying out the text by hand with a pencil

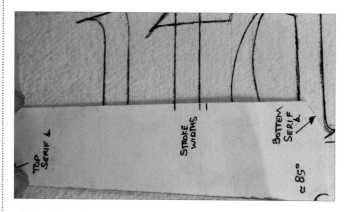

Checking the angles

DESIGN CONSIDERATIONS

Think carefully about where the finished carving will be placed. It must sit comfortably within the location, whether that is a modern apartment or an old church. Take care with the sizing of the lettering to make sure it will blend in, unless of course your intention is to make it stand out.

There are hundreds of different lettering styles; although you may have your personal favourites, make sure the style you choose suits the project. Sharp, jazzy lettering would be out of place in a calm environment, for example. Equally, a delicate copperplate script would not be suitable for advertising a disco event. Lettering, like music, can connect with a period in time and a location, Hector Guimard's classic 'Metropolitan' sign (*c.* 1900) typifies French Art Nouveau, for example.

Faded but still beautiful

If you are carving with wood, the grain can have a serious impact on carved letters, either enhancing or distracting from the design, so this needs to be seriously considered. Lettering can also be overpowered by elaborate detail. You need to think about the design in its entirety, rather than just plucking out design elements that you like and throwing them all into the mix together.

Make sure that the technical aspects of your lettering do not let you down. If it's a formal work, the stroke widths all need to be the same and the letters should be upright, not leaning. Letters such as 'A', 'M' and 'W' should not look like structures that are about to topple over. Ensure that the letters all appear to be the same size and that the spacing is correct. Do not focus on one section to the exclusion of the overall piece. When carving, make sure that you are focused on the shape and form of the letter; do not just concentrate on your carving skills. Brilliantly cut but incorrect letter shapes are still incorrectly cut letters, unless the design specifically calls for different-sized letters.

▶   *A carved inscription in slate by David Holgate*

COMMISSIONS

To enable you to produce a satisfactory piece of commissioned work, there has to be a meeting of minds between you and the client. Start by asking the following questions:

- Size or shape constraints
- Type of materials required
- Size of materials required
- Preferred lettering style
- The client's budget.

If there is a size constraint, make sure the desired inscription will fit. If there are too many words to be carved, the letter size may be too small to hand carve, and probably therefore too expensive to even attempt. Make sure you get all of this information in writing to protect yourself from any problems that may arise.

Produce a scale drawing for the client, the highest quality you can achieve. If they accept this and your quote, ask them to pay a deposit, look for any errors such as spelling mistakes and then ask the client to sign the work off.

BRUSH & PEN TECHNIQUES

ALTHOUGH I have dabbled in calligraphy using a pen, for design letter work I still prefer to use a brush, chalk and pencil when constructing my designs. To develop your letter drawing skills, you will need to set aside hours of practice time, probably accompanied by hours of frustration, before achieving satisfactory levels of consistency and proficiency. The good news is, that although this can be frustrating at times, it can also be very pleasing and is a rewarding thing to do. It has the bonus that practice is never wasted, and a natural understanding of the letterforms can start to be developed.

If you have been working with tools for a while, turning your attention to a project requiring drawing, painting or a lettering design can often be slightly problematic. To get into the mood, I will often pick up the drawing tools and doodle in a sketchbook, practising letterforms and various strokes; this definitely focuses the attention and gets me into 'the zone'.

Brush-influenced letterforms are an important part of the projects produced within this book. If I have a mental block or lack of ideas in the initial stages of the design process, picking up the paintbrushes and practising a few strokes helps to focus my attention and pull me back on track. The following techniques and exercises are designed to introduce you to this fascinating process. Enjoy.

FOR ALL TECHNIQUES

A drawing board set at an angle of about 60°, or a multi-slope with light window attachment, or a light box

FOR BRUSH TECHNIQUE

Watercolour or good-quality paper
Chisel-ended paintbrushes
Watercolour paint
Ceramic pallet or similar paint-mixing dish
Container for water
Masking tape

FOR PEN TECHNIQUE

Dip pens of varying widths
A small paintbrush for ink transferral
Ink stick and grinding container
Large paperclips
Smooth, good-quality paper

FOR TRANSITION

Tracing paper
6H pencil
HB pencil
Eraser
Smooth, good-quality paper
Scalpel
Abrasive paper/nail file
Conté crayons
Charcoal
Glue

ADDITIONAL EQUIPMENT

Geometrical equipment such as a protractor and a wooden square
A pair of compasses
Drawing pins
Photocopier

Dab the brush to spread the bristles and produce a sharp edge

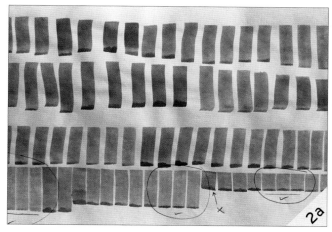

Vertical practice lines with the brush

Horizontal practice lines

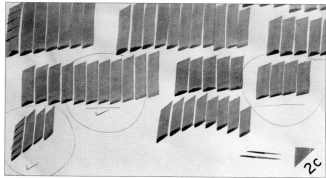

Vertical practice strokes, picking out the better ones

BRUSH TECHNIQUE

Painting letters can be done either sitting or standing, but when standing you have a wider range of movement, thus giving you an element of freedom in your designs. Use a light touch and fluid action with no tension present.

There are several techniques for holding the brush. I tend to favour an upright position with or without the outside pad of the hand touching or lightly brushing the paper. When painting standing up, I often use a flourishing technique with a type of pantographic action from the shoulder. Experiment to find the most comfortable position for you. The more adept and familiar you become with the brush, the greater your flexibility and experimentation will become. The only real 'given' as far as I am concerned is that the brush should be held very lightly – no white knuckles, please.

1 Mix the watercolour paint to a light creamy consistency, then load your brush. Dab the brush onto the paper until a sharp chisel edge is achieved. A reservoir of paint should still be present within the brush to create the stroke.

2 Start to form brushstrokes using a relaxed, controlled, even action. Here, I am holding the brush at a 45° angle (the cant). Enjoy the action and the resultant marks. Practise vertical, horizontal and vertical stroke mark making (**a**), (**b**), (**c**).

When it feels right you do not even need to look; try closing your eyes and feel the weight of the paint in the brush; feel the contact of the bristles on the paper.

Tip Your muscles have a memory, 'a recording of a right action'. If you try walking, safely, in the dark, your feet tell you the surface you are on. Shut your eyes and touch different surfaces with the tips of your fingers: you can recognise them and other objects. Eyes are only a part of 'seeing'; trust your other senses.

Practice letter strokes

Serif practice with the brush, circling the good examples

Changing the angle or cant of the brush changes the letter

Changing the colour of the paint extends the life of the practice paper and can give a pleasing effect

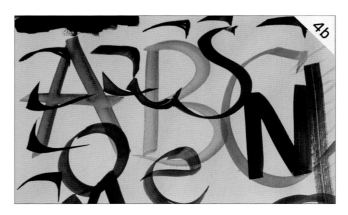

Going from a weaker mix of paint to a stronger one gives a pleasing effect as well as extending the life of the practice paper

3 Practise curved strokes (**a**), (**b**). Change the angle of cant and note the effect it has on a letter (**c**).

4 Experiment by using a slightly weaker mix of paint in a particular colour, by changing to another tube in a different colour or using a thicker mix of paint. Doing this will extend the life of the practice paper and creates pleasing effects and designs (**a**), (**b**).

Feel the weight of the paint-filled bristles and deftly handle the brush

Feel the curve and vary the pressure on the brush

You can form beautiful three-dimensional effects

Adding charcoal or pencil lines to brushstrokes can enhance them

PAPER CHOICE

When you're starting out, you are going to get through a lot of paper so you will want to use the cheapest that is suitable. Any paper will do as long as it can hold the wet paint or ink without disintegrating. However, once your technique improves, it's worth spending a little extra money and switching to good-quality paper. Calligraphers require a smooth paper with a 'tooth' or edge so that the letters are sharp. You may require larger paper too – A3 is recommended, rather than A4. Remember to date and store your work so tha you can create a useful record of your progress.

5 The strokes making up the structure of the letter will narrow and widen as they are formed by the action of your brush. The design of the letter stroke is determined by the angle and orientation of the brush and the varying rates of speed that occur when you change direction and lift the brush off the page at the end of the stroke. Generally, a slow movement of the brush results in a thicker line; the faster you go the thinner the line becomes (**a**), (**b**).

6 You can produce some beautiful, almost three-dimensional effects using the brush as it starts to run out of paint.

7 Use a charcoal stick or a pencil to outline some of the strokes or letters to enhance them and remove unwanted wobbles.

Roughing out the drawn letter using a Conté crayon

Tracing and modifying the letter

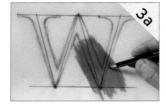

Tracing shows the internal structure

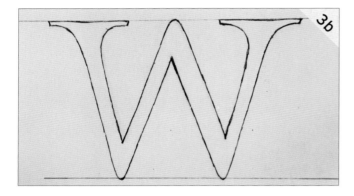

The finished letter 'W'

'W'

1 Using a piece of Conté crayon, form the structure of the 'W' by visually interpreting the brushstrokes (b, see box, right). I did this freehand but you could use tracing paper to start off with if you wish.

2 Take a piece of lining paper and a pencil, then carefully draw over this interpretation.

3 Reposition it over a blank piece of paper (**a**) and trace it onto that, adding the internal skeleton lines for this letter. When this drawing is finished, keep it as a record alongside the original brushed letter, until you are ready to carve it (**b**).

EXTRA PRACTICE

The letter 'C' and the letter 'W' were produced using a chisel-ended brush held in one orientation (a), (b). The letters 'ABC' were randomly painted onto a sheet of paper in red watercolour paint (c). The letter 'W' was then redrawn for the purpose of carving onto a piece of wood or stone at a future date, while the 'ABC' letters will be used as the basis of a print design. Using scrap pieces of hardwood and poor quality plywood, some brush letters were applied in different colours (d). See pages 78–101 for more details about the carving processes for wood and stone.

The letters 'C' and 'W' reconstructed with brushstrokes

Highlighting a stroke on the letter 'A' and edging in the letter 'C'

Random letters on scrap wood for painting and carving practice

Cutting out the photocopied letters

The letters are positioned, then glued down

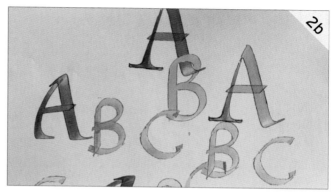

Some letters are linked, an interesting feature that will enhance carving

Photocopy the finished design

'ABC'

1 Make photocopies of your painted letters, some in black and white and the rest in colour. Cut these copies into randomly selected letters or groups of the letters 'ABC'.

2 Position the letters onto a blank sheet of paper and shuffle them around until a design starts to emerge (**a**). If you look closely at my design you will start to see that there are flow lines present: some curved, both vertical and horizontal. (**b**).

3 When you're satisfied, glue your design into place and photocopy it ready to use in a future printing block project. (Don't forget to reverse the image, though.)

The pen drawing equipment laid out

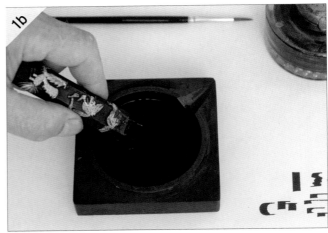

Grinding the ink can be therapeutic

A second-hand blotter propped up by a piece of wood, used as a writing slope

The dip pen being primed with ink

Holding the pen primed with ink

PEN TECHNIQUE

1 Sit at a desk or slope set at a comfortable angle. Add a prepared surface of blotting paper, padded underneath to allow a little 'give' to help when using the pen. I prefer to grind my own ink as it helps me to 'set the scene', but use shop-bought ink if you prefer (**a**), (**b**).

2 Attach a sheet of good-quality smooth writing paper.

3 Use a small paintbrush to apply the ink to the dip pen rather than dipping the pen into the ink pot.

4 With a fully primed pen, make contact with the paper using a sideways action to encourage ink flow, then start writing. I find using a dip pen extremely helpful for giving an insight into the letter structure. And of course, the more you practice the more understanding you will achieve.

5 Practise the letters 'ABC' (**a**). With some photographic technological help and possibly some tweaking with a pencil or draughtsman's pen at a later date, this can be a template for a block or screen print (**b**), (**c**).

6 This letter 'r' was produced alongside many others during a couple of hours' practice with a pen. I added lines to the paper on this particular occasion, four nib widths apart.

Tip The standard of your work won't be good enough to proceed to writing calligraphic script (this requires hundred of hours of practice) but as carvers we often produce work consisting of just a few words or letters, so we can cherry pick the 'good' ones. Having perhaps now completed the 'S' and 'A' practice exercises in this book, why not print off my penned 'r', modify it, then use it for further carving practice? Or try penning your own letters, change and adapt them, then carve them.

Watercolour paper with practice brush marks and added pen letters

A possible template for a block or screen print

The letters turned into a black-and- white image to be used for a print

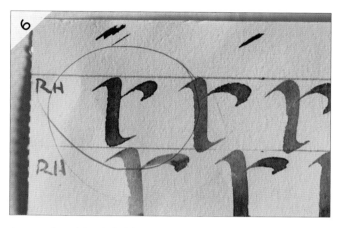

A practice letter 'r' is plucked from the range of practice letters

THE TRANSITION STAGE

To take your painted or inked letter and transpose it onto a piece of wood or stone you will need a pencil with a long point formed by a scalpel then finished off carefully with sandpaper or a file. If you are using an unmodified painted letter, you can correct or fine-tune it by drawing around it with a fine pen or pencil. You can then either paint or draw the letter directly onto the wood or stone, or trace the letter onto the material. For the latter option, take a suitably sized strip of detail or tracing paper (see page 34) and rub your chosen medium onto it in an even covering. If you're tracing onto stone, use soft charcoal or graphite for creamy limestone and soft white chalk or crayon for slate.

It is very easy to believe that the tracing you have taken, even after careful preparation, is a totally accurate representation of the original painted letter or line drawing it was taken from. Unfortunately if you carefully but slavishly follow the lines whilst tracing the original letter, the copy you produce, whilst

looking similar, may in fact be full of technical inaccuracies and possibly an unpleasing representation. The way that I approach this transition stage is to treat the faint line tracing produced on the wood or stone as a guide only. Then whilst carefully examining the original dawn or painted letter I attempt to redraw the script as an improved version of the original. At every stage including the carving one this concept is followed, always trying to improve on the previous one.

GUIDE MARKS
In order to position the drawing onto the timber, cut out a small section of the tracing paper drawing at intersection points and match these to designated points on your timber (see page 122). These should line up perfectly, which means that removing the drawing any time is not a problem.

Further practice

AMPERSAND

THE AMPERSAND has been around for more than 2,000 years. It is a symbol that originated as a ligature of the letters 'et' (the Latin for 'and'). The textbooks often tell us that minuscule letters were derived from majuscule over a long period of time, the logic behind this being the necessity to write quickly in order for daily life to proceed at a regular pace. The changing letters eventually end up in a form that trips lightly off the pen with speed and ease. I am sure that to a certain extent this is true. I do not think, however, that this theory takes into account the artistic sensibilities, skills or opinions of the people who over millennia have produced beautiful and often complicated text. I have spent hours trying to perfect brushed letter construction, part of an addiction I still enjoy. I am convinced that far from being accidental or developed purely through necessity, beautiful letterforms in general, and the ampersand in particular, were designed for aesthetic reasons as well.

Brushed letter formation is often frustrating and at times satisfactory results are unachievable. But when you 'nail it' and a beautiful letterform is presented in front of you, constructed with two or three strokes, there is a great feeling of satisfaction and release. In this practice session, the brush stays at the same angle (cant) for strokes 1 and 2. The only time it changes is on stroke 3 at the start where I have shown the twist.

ITC Berkeley Oldstyle (this book's font)

ITC Berkeley Oldstyle Italic

Adobe Caslon Italic

MATERIALS

Good-quality watercolour paper

A selection of high-quality chisel-ended brushes

Paint mixing pots

Masking tape

A drawing board set at an angle of about 60°,

or a multi-slope with light window attachment,

or a light box

Tracing paper

HB pencil

Photocopier

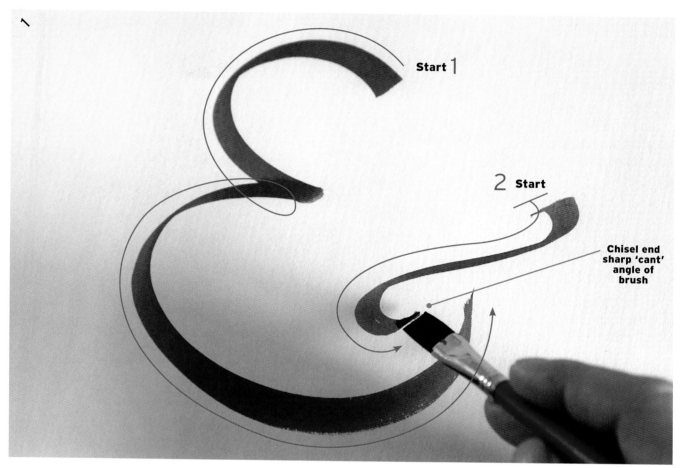

Loosening up with the 2 stroke – 'et'

Start 1

2 Start

Chisel end
sharp 'cant'
angle of
brush

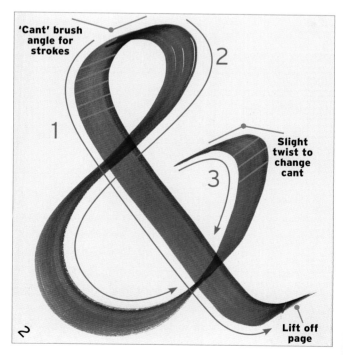

'Cant' brush
angle for
strokes

Slight
twist to
change
cant

Lift off
page

The ampersand is produced with three brushstrokes

PRACTISE

1 A good starting point is to loosen up and practise the two strokes associated with the word 'et'. This after all was the starting point for the ampersand's form and I hope you can see the similarities in the construction of the two symbols. The 'et' symbol has a very italic feel in its construction, and it clearly shows the infinite variation in stroke width achievable by a brush when held at one angle of cant for the duration of the stroke. It flows from the thinnest to the thickest achievable brushstroke with ease, with a loop of the brush in the middle of the first stroke. Practise this before starting the ampersand.

2 Scan or photocopy the photograph of the finished ampersand and attach it to your light box or the multi-slope light window. The construction of this monogram is with three independent brushstrokes. After hours of lettering practice (see Brush techniques, pages 62–7), you should be familiar with the requirements and brushstroke techniques needed to construct this symbol.

Practice makes perfect

Relax into the zone

3 Moving a piece of watercolour paper over the attached ampersand symbol on the light box will allow you to fill up the whole paper with your early attempts at getting to grips with the brushwork. Changing the colour and then the dilution of the paint means that you can still see individual strokes and extend the life of the paper.

STROKE 1

4 This sets the scene for the strength and ultimately the success of the symbol. Relax and start thinking your way into the letterform. Load your brush with paint and dab the brush on the paper, setting the sharp chisel-ended point needed to start the curve. Starting at the top of the curve, point 'x', run down the straight at the correct angle. If you are nervous or tense the stroke will 'wobble' and be inconsistent. As you reach the bottom of the curve, it slows up and the stroke thickens slightly. Lift the brush as you turn the corner to speed things up again, producing the thin pointed finish as the brush leaves the paper (y).

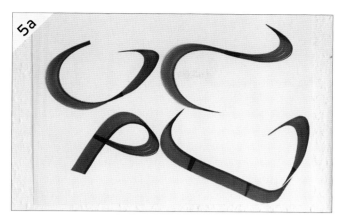

The constructing strokes

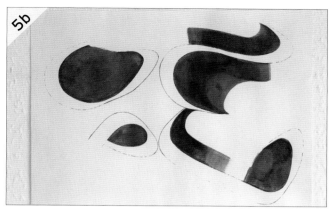

The negative spaces of the constructing strokes

Line drawing for tracing, then carving

The final 12

STROKE 2

Reload and dab the brush again and then start the reverse 'S' stroke (y). You may find this part easier and, with the correct flourish and spontaneity, it will become an elegant and beautifully curved shape. Aim for the point where this stroke meets and then crosses the first stroke; lift the brush off the page as you are about to cross over it.

STROKE 3

5 The pressure is back on again with the last stroke (z), especially if the first two strokes worked out well. Set the brush angle to horizontal, and then start twisting it as you move down with the stroke until you arrive at the normal angle or cant. This angle is then used for the remainder of the stroke. Your aim is to meet up with the stroke 'y' as it crosses stroke 'x', but you must also be aware of the curves you are producing (**a**), (**b**). Keep practising until your '&' looks good.

6 You now have a working design that can be used as a template for a carving on either wood or stone. Using this you can produce your own line drawing and thus proceed to the carving stage. I have however produced a copy for you to use of my own line drawing, if you would like to bypass this stage.

CONCLUSION

7 I like to sort out the practice sheets into graded piles, normally marked out of 10. I will often add comments, but always add dates. These sheets become a useful record of progress made. I hope when referring to it you will see a vast improvement in your skill levels.

SHARPENING CHISELS

I HAVE USED fifteen modern chisels and gouges, four Victorian carving chisels, an old Carpenter's chisel and three letter-cutting tools to produce all the exercises and projects in the book. The grain issues in wood are the reason why you need far more chisels than when working with stone. The wood chisels fall into three different groups: 'V' cut or parting tools, curved gouges and skew chisels. The three stone chisels are similar but with differing widths.

All of the tools used in this book were brand-new, and arrived beautifully sharpened. But don't assume that spanking new tools are fit for purpose – this may not always be the case, so learning how to sharpen your tools correctly is essential.

No matter how experienced or proficient you are, if you use poorly sharpened tools, all sorts of problems will arise, and as a consequence you will produce substandard work. If you have second-hand tools, rust will be the main problem.

If you are an experienced carver I'm sure you will have a sharpening system in place. For those who do not I have tried to reduce to a minimum a sharpening system that can be used anywhere and involves no electrical power, only elbow grease. It can be used for all of the chisels, using a combination of abrasive diamond strips, natural stones and a leather strop to complete the task. I spend more time sharpening wood chisels than stone-carving ones, honing them to a razor-sharp edge.

YOU WILL NEED
Diamond strips of different grades
Oil stone
Slipstones
Leather strops

Tip If sharpening is a new experience for you I suggest you join a friendly woodcarving organisation for help and support. Buy some old tools and then it's practice, practice, practice until you feel confident in what you're doing.

The sharpening station laid out

Using a diamond strip

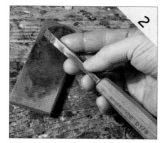

Gently holding the chisel

Any size oil stone will do

The candle

A home-made leather strop

No candle, so just a strop with the leather required

METAL REMOVAL

1 Decide on the level of sharpening needed to render a tool fit for purpose. If this is a full resharpen, for example, as is often the case with old or second-hand tools, then you will need to start removing metal. To do this job effectively by hand I use diamond strips of varying grades attached to a block of oak for ease of use. The block can then be held in a vice, leaving both your hands free to continue with the sharpening.

2 I use oil stones after the diamond strips. There are several sharpening jigs on the market but I suggest you just hold the tool and start removing metal. I tend to press down with a finger near the sharpening edge with my other hand not gripping in any way but just being used as support, no white knuckles.

3 I generally push forwards when sharpening but on occasion will move the tool from side to side, often rolling it when sharpening curved gouges. Move the chisel around the oil stone to distribute the wear. Oil for lubrication is a good idea, but always follow the manufacturer's instructions.

4 On rusty curved gouges, always remove all the rust from the inside edge first, bringing the surface to an almost complete finish. Sharpen the outside bevel next, always looking to remove every sign of the glinting light on the cutting edge of the tool, known as the candle.

5 Be quite specific in the areas that you sharpen. If you see no candle then it's already sharp enough; just a strop is all that is required! If you spot minute sections of candle still glinting, revert back to your finest grade oil stone, and concentrate on the areas that need work. Follow with a quick strop using the leather (**a**), and the chisel should be ready for use (**b**).

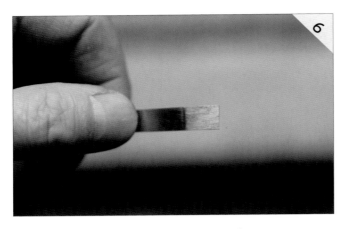

The roughened appearance before the slipstones are used

Gently polishing the tool using a small slipstone; take care not to cut yourself

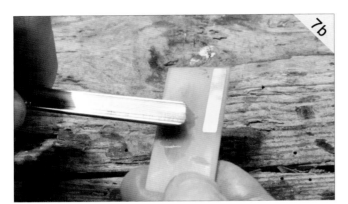

Carefully fine-tuning a 'V' tool

If the curve fits then this can be a useful stone

STAGES OF FINISHING

6 When you have removed all signs of rust the two surfaces should meet and form a burr. You can feel this with your fingernail.

7 Using a series of differently graded oil- and slipstones, you will end up with a razor sharp cutting edge, the junction where the two polished surfaces meet (**a**), (**b**), (**c**).

8 In the process of sharpening the tool the burr will naturally break off. You can often see this floating in the oil present on the oil stones.

The burr breaks off

A home-made leather strop

Testing the edge on a piece of old pine

The edge appears crumbly; maybe rust is still there

A useful method to hone small 'V' tools

Folded over leather useful for honing inside 'V' tools

THE FINAL HONE

9 Using leather strops, either home-made or shop-bought, and without applying too much pressure, start stropping.

10 Double check for any candle and test the cutting edge. I suggest you keep a piece of old pine next to your sharpening station for this purpose.

11 Chisels such as 'V' tools require a delicate touch when sharpening, 'Hooks' at the thicker junction of the cutting edges can occur if you are not careful. Think of this tool as three separate chisels: two flat ones, 'the sides' and a small curved one at the bottom of the 'V'.

12 To hone small 'V' tools, cut a groove into a piece of wood using the particular tool, then apply some metal polish. Run it backwards and forwards in this groove to hone the outside edge. Turn it upside down and produce a couple of furrows with metal polish applied to then hone the inside edge.

13 To hone the inside edge of large curved gouges and 'V' tools, use differently shaped pieces of wood with a piece of leather wrapped around, or stuck on. A folded over and clamped piece of leather can also be used to strop these edges.

STONE CARVING CHISELS
We are only using three letter carving chisels within this book; straight edged with secondary bevels applied. They have a tungsten carbide tip and require very little work to remain fit for purpose. If they're straight from the factory they may just require a quick tweak on the diamond blocks. Otherwise it's the same procedure for removing metal as for woodcarving chisels, except that the angle of the secondary bevel will vary according to the thickness of the tool and the hardness of the material it is cutting.

WOODCARVING TECHNIQUES

To DEMONSTRATE these techniques I used a piece of pitch pine (*Pinus rigida*) of mediocre quality. You will note from the photographs how brittle and resinous the winter growth rings were with the summer growth being particularly spongy and soft. Handle the timber and feel the different textures with your finger tips. Look at any anomalies and get to know the timber. Start thinking about how you can work with it and bring it under control if necessary!

This is an ideal practice material but you will need razor-sharp chisels for good results. There is no easy way to achieve these techniques other than to practice, but they will become second nature after a while. You can if you wish modify this section to include several different types of wood to practise upon. They may have varying hardness and density of grain, differing types of imperfections to deal with including knots, minor shakes and larger splits, for example. By replicating the carving techniques in this section on each practice piece of wood comparisons can be made, mistakes corrected, and further experience gained.

A set of well-sharpened chisels

CARVING TOOLS
Firmer: D1/8
'V' parting tools: D12/2, 12/8, 12/10
Skew chisels: D1S/8, D1S/12
Curved chisels: 3/22, D5/12, D5/8, D8/10, D8/4, 5F/8
Dummy/mallet c. 1lb (460g) in weight

ADDITIONAL EQUIPMENT
HB pencil
Metal rule, 12in (30cm)
Plastic curves

BEST PRACTICE TECHNIQUES
Other than the usual health and safety considerations (see pages 46–7), there are no rules or constraints with these techniques. The only suggestions I will make are:
- Cut cleanly and accurately at all times
- Experiment with as many different strokes as you can, with every different type of gouge that you own
- Cut with the grain, across the grain and against the grain
- Don't box yourself into a corner with small, tight carving, unless with deliberate intent
- Try some long sweeping curves: it's good to free yourself up sometimes
- Focus on the things you find most difficult, but don't labour over them
- Don't turn this practice into a project and become too precious about it

Familiarise yourself with the mallet; it should be a comfortable grip

The grip for paring; the little finger acts as the break

Mallet work: no white knuckles

Paring, both hands working in unison

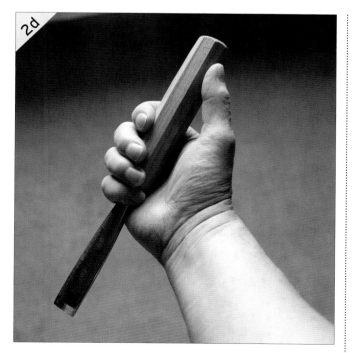

The grip used when working with the mallet

FAMILIARITY AND CONFIDENCE

1 Place the mallet in the palm of your hand, then move it around, passing it from hand to hand, rolling it between your fingers, testing the weight and trying out the grip that best suits you. The head of the mallet is circular for a reason; it ensures effective contact with a chisel or gouge, which means that you don't have to keep checking its position. You should be observing the point at which the cutting surface of the tool joins the material to be carved at all times.

2 Having chosen which particular chisel you wish to practice with, place it in the palm of your hand (**a**). Roll the handle between your thumb and fingers – you should be able to keep turning it through 360° in both directions and in both hands. The object of this exercise is the familiarisation necessary to encourage a firm but light touch. When you feel comfortable, and both hands and tools are starting to work together, it is time to cut some timber (**b**), (**c**), (**d**).

Gently chasing up the curve using progressively larger gouges

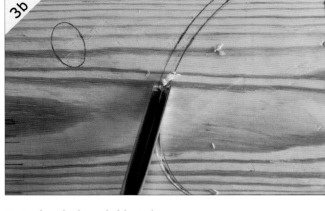

Moving from the thin end of the stroke...

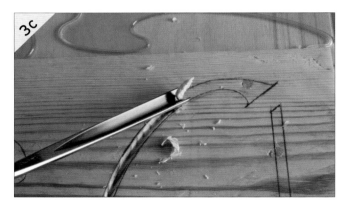

... to the thickest

Completing the chasing up and the beginning of the chip cut

THE 'V' TOOL

REMOVING WOOD

Attach your timber to the Multi-slope or carving bench and draw as many shapes relating to the lettering projects as you can think of. If you feel confident, draw by hand; if not, use French curves, compasses and a rule.

3 Begin carving the first shape using the mallet and three different-sized 'V' tools, proceeding from the thin end of the stroke to the thickest (**a**), (**b**), (**c**), (**d**). You will notice that I didn't draw a centreline through the sweeping curve. It is good practice to rely on your vision and hand skills to complete the task. Image (**e**) is a freehand sketch of useful shapes with centrelines added, to help you visualize your own.

This process is all about removing wood, starting from the centre and working out to the sides. The further apart the lines are, the deeper you will need to cut, which is why you need to increase

Adding the centrelines

the size of the chisel you use as you proceed upwards. However, don't be tempted to cut too deeply at this stage; you should not yet cut to the bottom of the 'V' cut you have drawn.

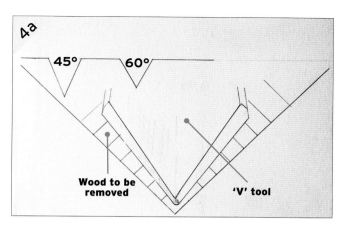

The optimum angle of cut

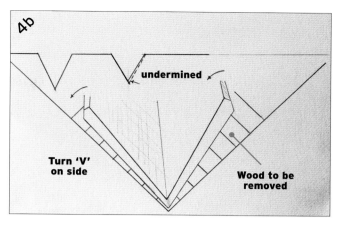

Tilt the 'V' tool to open out the cut

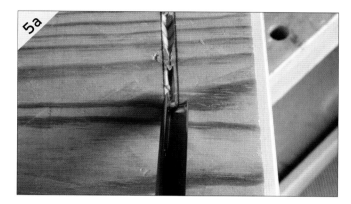

Only remove half the pencil line

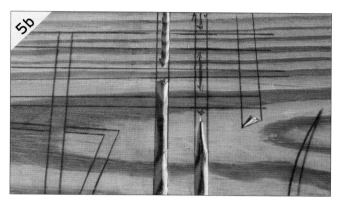

It's all about control: try not to overshoot the line

4 This demonstrates what I consider to be the optimum angle of cut: between 45° and 60° (**a**), (**b**). Don't get too hung up on angles though; you will naturally produce your own that will suit. Look at your progress from all angles; decide how much deeper you need to go and whether you need to make any adjustments.

OPENING OUT THE CUT

5 To start the process of opening out the 'V' cut, you need to tilt the 'V' tool as shown in 4a and 4b. Although this means cutting deeper, you can see that I have left enough of a margin of error to allow for the extra wood removal needed during finishing (**a**). Run up one side to open it out (**b**), then finish off by running up the other side.

Chase up the curve and visualise the junction

A difficult curve, but good practice!

THE SKEW CHISEL

Having safely removed as much timber as possible using the 'V' tools, it is now time to get to grips with the sometimes difficult but extremely versatile skew chisel. For now, you will not use any other curved gouges during these practice exercises.

MAKING A CHIP CUT

6 First, cut a chip cut within a curved shape, referring back to images 4a and 4b. Starting at the end of the serif and with the skew angled outwards, chase up the centreline using the heel of the skew and the mallet (**a**). Think of the heel cutting down, aiming towards the junction at the bottom of the 'V' cut. Repeat this on the other side. This is a difficult curve and may even be against the grain. Gently tap the skew chisel and cut along the drawn line, again heading down to meet at the junction (**b**).

Tip Tapping the skew gently and lifting the heel slightly as you cut around curves will enable you to produce tight curves - they will become tighter and tighter with practice. Don't forget that this is just a familiarizing exercise. Curved gouges are introduced as and when required.

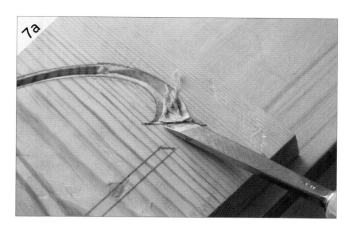

You will now find out whether the sides meet

The point of the skew is often useful at this stage

Use curved gouges if necessary

Chasing up an accurate centreline

The difficult outer curve

7 Still using the heel of the skew, cut the third side of the triangular shape, with the visual image in mind (**a**). You may have to repeat this a couple of times to remove the chip. The point of the skew can be used at this stage, just be careful not to dig into the side wall of the letter, as this would be difficult to rectify later (**b**). When the triangular piece of wood pops out, remove the remaining section with the point of the skew. Note that because of the nature of this curve, I would normally use the circular gouge D5/12 to assist (**c**).

TIDYING UP

8 Starting from the thin end of the stroke and gently using the mallet, finish off the 'V' cut (**a**), (**b**). There are four important points to follow here:

- Make sure the heel of the skew is running along the bottom of an accurate centreline.
- Adjust your angle of cut to be the same for both sides.
- Check that you are running accurately between the lines.
- Aim to cut away only half of the pencil line.

Opening out with the skew, first left …

… then right

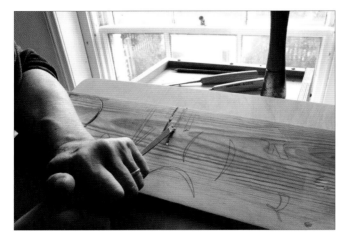

Carving by hand, comfortably in control

Control between the junctions

LESSONS IN CONTROL

9 To help with the control process, a good place to start is by turning your work upside down. This will give you a different visual perspective, and avoid over-familiarization with letter shapes and 'meanings'. These exercises are not about that. Cut out a random series of shapes with and without the mallet. Try to get into a rhythm and accept that mistakes will be made. Move on. Don't become too wrapped up in a particular area of carving as this is all about fluency and acquiring expertise. A cut across the grain is easier to control at a junction so I suggest that you begin your practice running with the grain, but of course, also practice against it to achieve equal control. Use a stop cut for vulnerable areas when necessary, but as you think your way into the work you may find that the order you tackle things naturally produces these cuts. The main thing to remember is that both hands need to be working in unison; if you are working without the mallet the hand holding the chisel acts as a kind of brake to stop you running too far forwards when you need to stop at the junction.

Try to stay relaxed. Tensions in your body can lead to wobbles and mistakes in your carving. Take a break if necessary before continuing with the practice. When you are ready to start again check your tools for maximum sharpness, often a major cause of frustration and failure if blunt.

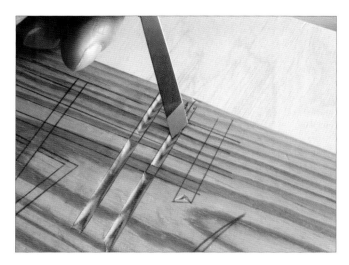

A finishing touch

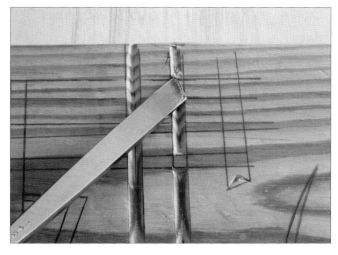

Aim towards the centre and bottom of the 'V' when cutting a chip

I usually start with the smaller widths at an intersection

Take care to avoid splitting any corners

Check your progress; don't continue with poorly executed or untidy work

With a 'tap' too far, the chip has overrun

If unsure at complicated junctions, start drawing

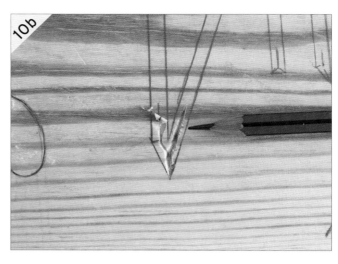

A poorly sharpened chisel leads to crumbling edges!

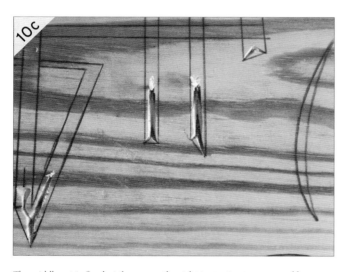

The middle cut is fine but the one on the right is starting to cause problems, leading to the big problem junction

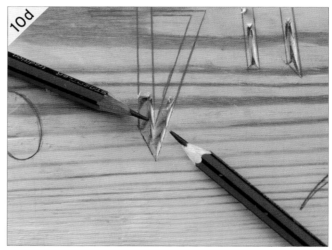

Trying to correct the damage caused by a blunt tool often leads to an escalation in problems; such as slope angle variance

ANALYSING PROBLEM JUNCTIONS

10 For problem junctions, draw in the centre lines (**a**). My 'V' tool was losing its edge as I carved this, so it's a good opportunity to flag up the difference that even a slightly blunt tool can make to the work and the additional time it adds to the project if not addressed. The first sign of a blunt tool is that wood becomes crumbly (**b**). Pieces are likely to fall off, which can then lead to design issues. Compare this with the carving in (**c**), for which I sharpened the tool. The two newly carved sections are of a far better quality. In (**d**) however, I cut away too much material in trying to save the triangular apex piece of short-grain wood and ended up with incorrectly angled sloping sides.

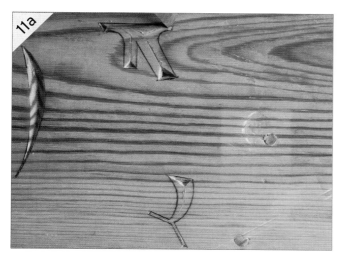

At a complicated junction, starting with the centre lines, followed by ends

Start with the tricky finishing first

Gently remove timber at vulnerable apex junctions

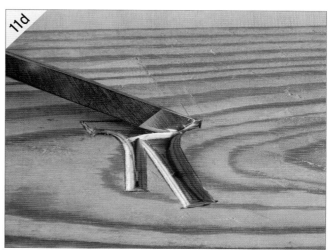

The heel of the skew is ideal for this cut

CARVING DIFFICULT JUNCTIONS

11 For carving difficult junctions, begin by gently cutting the centre lines with the skew (**a, b**). A good option for the next step is to complete the ends of the shape with chip cuts, which I have done here (**c**). If the carving is part of a larger design, start cutting the thin strokes first, then work towards the thicker ones, especially where junctions are concerned (**d, e**).

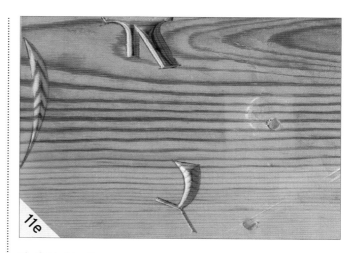

The finished junctions

The gouges needed for chasing out a thin oval

Expanding the 'V' cut

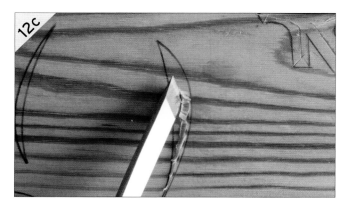

Cutting circular shapes just using the skew

Continuing the curve with the skew

USING SHAPED GOUGES

12 Chasing around a letter shape with a skew chisel means you don't need to have a large selection of shaped gouges in your tool roll. However when you have an understanding of the letterform, this should mean that where appropriate you will use the correctly shaped chisel to continue the letter in a seamless fashion around a difficult curve. The six curved gouges I have selected were enough to help complete all the projects and exercises in the book. It's always a good idea with a limited selection of tools to try to adapt the design of the letters to allow you to use particular chisels in particular sections. One example is the letter 'O'. I used the two gouges shown to carve this shape (**a**). With a small, thin curve it's quite possible to open out the 'V' by angling the gouge backwards while cutting (**b**), still aiming for the bottom of the 'V'. On the long curved stroke I used several of the curved gouges in the finishing stages (**c**), (**d**), (**e**).

Finishing with one of the curved gouges

RAISED LETTER 'S'

T HE TIMBER used for this exercise was part of a consignment of seasoned blocks destined for the wood burner. I split a log and trimmed the ends with a bandsaw, which gave me an irregular rectangular shaped block. The riven surface produced contained a variety of wild, undulating grain revolving around a knotty anomalous area. Other parts of the block had that particular yellow colouring consistent with the first signs of rot, and were rather crumbly. Even with all of these problems, it was a rather beautiful piece of wood. Woodturners are particularly fond of using spalted beech; the black lines where fungus has entered the wood and the differing colour variations make interesting turned objects. As letter carvers, however, we usually require a less lively

surface to allow the lettering to be seen. I therefore decided that a raised 'S' with the riven surface intact and a flatter background for contrast was the design I would use.

Raised lettering works best when the design contains bold and blocky lettering. Serifs are pretty much excluded from this type of work because they are extremely thin and vulnerable to breakage. I felt however that a delicate raised lettering design could be carved onto a piece of wood if the short grain issues were addressed. Please note that the ends of the letter are running with the grain, hence they are stronger, and should hopefully survive. The same letter carved onto a piece of stone may well be less durable.

CARVING CHISELS
Firmer: D1/8
'V' parting tool: 12/8
Flat skew chisels: D1S/12
Gouges: D5/12, D5/8, 3/22, 5F/8
Dummy/mallet

ADDITIONAL EQUIPMENT AND MATERIALS
Any timber you wish to carve
Scissors
Cramps
Wood and paper glue
Newspaper
Wooden batten
Multi-slope or carving stand
Detail paper/tracing paper
4B pencil/graphite
Photocopier

A glued paper joint will hold the work in position

Carefully cut out a paper template

Balance the position of the letter using your judgement

Carefully redraw the letter

CLAMPING THE TIMBER TO THE CARVING STAND

1 For this exercise, you will use a glued paper joint to clamp the timber. To do this, insert newspaper between the wood and a small ply batten, apply some glue and then clamp them together. As the surface was uneven, I inserted a wooden wedge for additional contact and support.

Add newspaper padding to the cramps to stop any bruising of the riven surface of the timber. Then apply a polyurethane foaming glue to fill any gaps where contact wasn't made. When secure, screw this arrangement onto the carving stand. After the carving is complete, the block can easily be removed from the batten by inserting a flat chisel and applying a quick tap with the mallet.

TRANSFERRING THE DESIGN TO THE TIMBER

2 If your timber has a flat surface, you can transfer the design using tracing paper and pencils, graphite sticks, Conté sticks or charcoal to rub onto it. When working with an uneven surface such as this, however, it's a good idea to photocopy the design and carefully cut it out with scissors or a scalpel to make a template. Try not to slavishly stick to the drawn line when cutting out this letterform. Refer to the original drawing and modify the letter if necessary with the scissors.

3 Position the cutout letter by eye onto the timber, then tack it onto the wood in a couple of places using a little water-based glue to hold it in place.

4 Carefully draw around the design using a soft charcoal pencil. This gives you a record of its position in case the photocopy gets dislodged. It also means that, if you want to increase the size of the letter, you can cut to the outside of this line.

Be aware of the shapes in the negative spaces

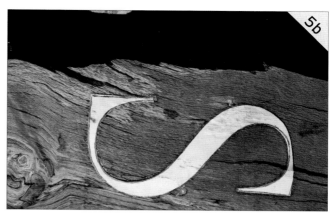

Ready to begin the carving

Use razor-sharp tools

Do not dig into the side of the letter

Reshape the letter

5 The orientation of the 'S' with the grain is up to you; there are no hard and fast rules as to the orientation of letters onto a carving surface. I chose to place the 'S' running parallel with the grain as I felt the extra protection offered to the ends of the serifs by avoiding the short grain issues was paramount. Also, from a design perspective this long letter was framed nicely within the rectangular shape of the block (**a**), (**b**).

CARVING

Whatever else you do, make sure your tools are razor sharp at all times. I had no idea how this piece of wood would react once I started to carve it, so decided upon a bold approach, but still allowed for a margin of error. The serif at the bottom of the 'S' was positioned over a crumbly section of timber next to the edge of a wooden cliff; care would need to be taken here. I decided to attack the more stable centre inside curve of the letter, heading northwards. Stabbing down with shaped gouges was not an option to start with, due to the fragile nature of the timber. I needed to relieve some of the pressure first.

6 Starting with the 'V' tool orientated slightly to the right, begin cutting a groove running parallel with the letter. This immediately drops the level and forms an outward angled wall, so be careful not to undercut (**a**). Once in place, this 'V'-shaped moat protects the letter and you can start to remove the waste next to it using a large 'off the flat' chisel (**b**). If the particular curve of the letter requires changing, your shaped gouges can come into play (**c**).

Take care at the corner

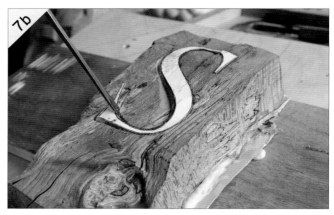

Do not apply any backward pressure to the letter

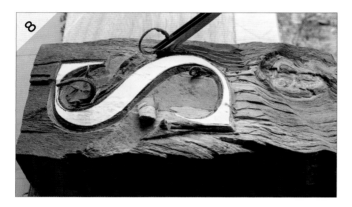

The 'V' tool can be very versatile

Do not cut into the side wall of the letter

7 Next, tackle the end of the letter, the bottom serif. Using a small firmer chisel and the skew, gently carve out the straight section of the shape, applying no pressure, and no mallet use. Take particular care at the corners. Set the inner curve in with the fishtail, then remove the waste using the firmer chisel (**a**), (**b**).

8 A good deal of the remaining carving will be done using the 'V' tool. Working the area below the letter, with the tool angled slightly on its side, cut away the background material until you reach the 'V'-cut 'moat' protecting the base of the letter. This way of working produces a tool-marked effect, rather than a flat cut finish.

9 Tip the 'V' tool completely over and run it parallel with the shape of the letter, not cutting into the letter wall, to remove most of the remaining base level material.

Tip At this stage it's payback time for all the previous long hours of practising with these versatile and adaptable tools. Feel confident in your own ability to use whichever tool you consider the most appropriate for the task, whether it be curved, straight or 'V'-shaped.

Do not get carried away and damage the letter

Adjusting the curve using a fish tail

Adjusting the inside curve of the letter

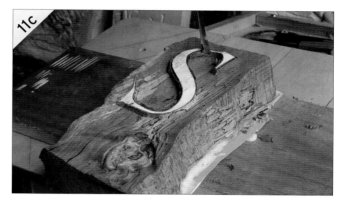

A different perspective of the letter, which is useful to see

The two gouges used to form this curve

10 The 'off the flat' fishtail is very effective in removing the remainder of this base material in the confines of the negative space at the top of the 'S'. Its lifted corners can cut right to the inside line of the curve of the letter.

11 The remainder of the work is done using a combination of all the different chisels and gouges. Use the shape of the letter, not the shape of the tool, to determine which tool should be used. This is particularly important when using a stab cut (**a**), (**b**), (**c**), (**d**).

Tip When stabbing down, only undercut if that is your intention. Otherwise the cut should be straight down at 90° to the base level.

STONE CARVING TECHNIQUES

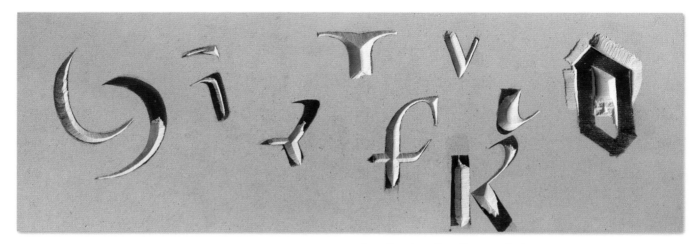

You will need an offcut of limestone for this practice

To DEMONSTRATE these stone carving techniques I used an offcut of prepared limestone which was 20in x 7¼in x 1in (510mm x 185mm x 25mm) thick. As this is a practice session, any limestone will do as long as it's clean with a prepared surface that will take watercolour paint.

ESSENTIAL TOOLS

Although stone does have grain, it does not have the same impact on the carving that wood grain has. In stone you can use one chisel, the rectangular square-ended tungsten carbide letter-cutting tool, to produce all of the lettering. Other types of lettering tools are available if you prefer, but this is my personal choice. For woodcarving, of course, you need many more tools to do the same job.

A claw chisel is often used for large raised letters with lots of background removal. As its name suggests, the claw consists of a set of sharpened metal triangular sections, instead of a straight cutting-edge. This chisel forms a series of parallel 'V' shaped grooves when carved through the stone. By firstly working in one direction and then rotating through 90° and carving again, small pyramids of stone are formed. These

can then be removed by continuing with the claw or using a normal chisel. The size of tool you use depends upon the width of the letterstrokes, which in turn dictates the depth of the 'V' cut. Ideally, the chisel, when in the cutting position and resting in the bottom of the 'V' cut centreline, should still be protruding above the top surface.

You will also need a stone carver's dummy (or a woodcarver's mallet, if you prefer). This should be used with a regular rhythm; take care to maintain this and try not to speed up.

CARVING TOOLS
TCT straight-edge lettering chisels: 3mm, 6mm and 10mm
Dummy/mallet

ADDITIONAL TOOLS AND MATERIALS
6H pencil
Chisel-ended paintbrush
Watercolour paint

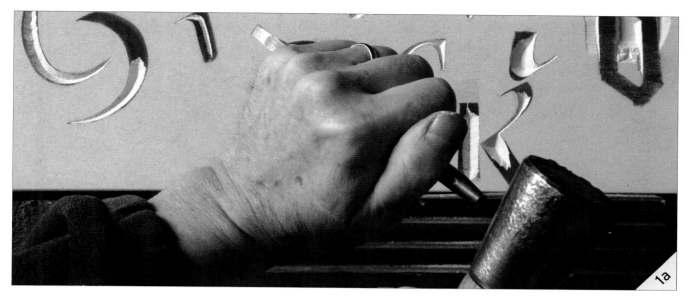

How to hold the chisel and the mallet

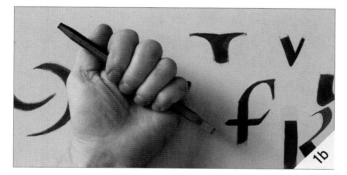

The correct grip for the stonecarving chisel

The starting cut

DRAW THE OUTLINES FIRST

To produce the lettering on the stone, draw the outlines of the letters with a hard pencil and then fill them in with watercolour paint. Alternatively, use a chisel-ended brush to paint the strokes directly on to the stone.

HOLDING THE TOOLS

1 The angle at which you hold the stone carving tool (**a**), dictates how effective you are: too shallow and you start to scrape, too upright and you start to dig in. Do not grip the tools too tightly (**b**). Allow the chisel to rest on the stone's surface. It will then start to cut and remove the high points and you will begin to feel the control given to you by the information it feeds back to you, almost as though the chisel is an extension of your sensitive fingertips. You are effectively cutting small steps of stone out of the 'V' cut section of the letter. These steps should be regular and clearly visible. Remember: no scraping!

STARTING TO CUT

2 Start at the thin end of a letter, such as the point of the serif, and gently develop the centreline. Don't start too aggressively as you could accidentally flake off pieces of stone larger than the confines of the letter shape. Accurate cutting at the start and setting in the centreline, determines the nature and appearance of the letter.

Tip Remember that this is only a practice exercise, so do not be too precious about the result. If it goes wrong, keep going, wash down the stone if necessary and start again.

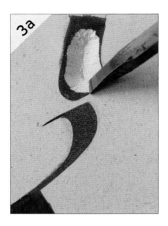

Shaping the centreline

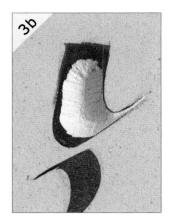

Gradually shaping the outside curve

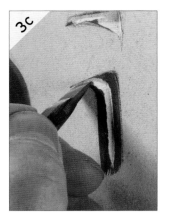

Finish fine strokes with a hand tool

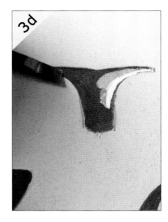

Carefully starting the cut...

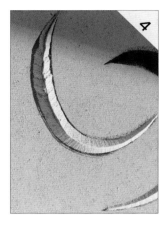

The chop marks used for quick stone removal can be seen here, next to the curve with a shallower angle of cut

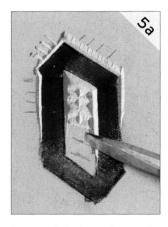

Lowering the background in raised lettering using a standard chisel

Breaking off the pyramids to lower the level

The bottom level has been set and the partially carved letter has differently angled sides and depths

3 Keep an awareness of the form of the letter and start to develop the 'V' cut both deeper and wider (**a**). Shape the letterstroke so it reflects the slightly differing curves of the inside and outside lines, while not forgetting the cleanly cut centreline (**b**). The end serif is usually a fine line, so it is often advisable to finish this gently by hand, without using a mallet (**c**), (**d**).

4 Using the chisel at a slightly steeper angle gives a more aggressive chop for quicker stone removal. The tooth-like marks this causes can be seen in the left-hand side curve. The right-hand side curved stroke has been partially finished using a shallower 'V' cut angle. This protects the sides of the letter from crumbling and is still capable of producing enough shadow to be effective as a carved letter.

5 Raised lettering (**a**) may often have slanted sides because of the vulnerability of the edges of the letter. For this practice carving you will only need to run a few crisscrossed 'V' cut lines using the standard tool (rather than a claw), (**b**) which should produce the necessary pyramid high points to allow the background to be accurately dropped. Once you have removed all of these small pyramids and tidied up, the depth can be reduced and the base level can be set (**c**).

Carve from thin into thick

Carving a junction

The completed junction of the letter 'K' – notice how the leg of the 'K' doesn't break into the upright stroke

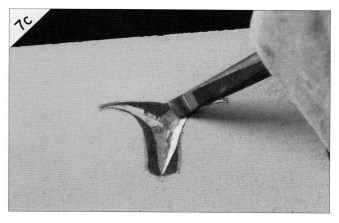

Work both serifs and the stem of the letter simultaneously

The tricky junction of the letter 'R'

CARVING THE JUNCTIONS

6 The junctions in stone carving have similar problems to those in woodcarving. As a general rule, carve the thin stroke first if the junction comprises of two dissimilar sized strokes meeting.

7 When joining together strokes of different widths and depths at a point, they need to be both pleasing to the eye and accurately represent the letterform they are producing. Take care not to break off any of the vulnerable pieces of stone present in the junction of the letters 'V' , 'F', 'R' and 'A', for example (**a**). The leg of the letter 'K' does not break into the upright stroke at the junction. This is a design feature and take care not to get too close, otherwise things may crumble and they may suddenly join together (**b**). Photograph (**c**) shows how the junction is carefully formed, cutting from three directions with the centreline in mind. Similarly the junction of the letter 'R' can be tricky, with three letterstrokes coming together (**d**).

INCISED 'V' CUT LETTER 'A'

Having read the stone carving techniques section of the book and practised on a few pieces of suitable stone, you are now in a position to attempt a project. I suggest you start on a small scale, carving a single letter. I have chosen a capital 'A', carved on a piece of slate. Draw your own design if you wish, or use a photocopy of the template I have provided. Make a few practice runs on scrap pieces of stone before moving on to a prepared piece of quality stone.

TOOLS AND EQUIPMENT

Stone carving chisels

TCT lettering chisels: 3mm, 6mm and 10mm

Dummy/mallet

A piece of natural/riven slate

Carving stand

C300 detail paper/tracing paper

6H pencil and hard white pencil or crayon

Tri-square

Photocopier

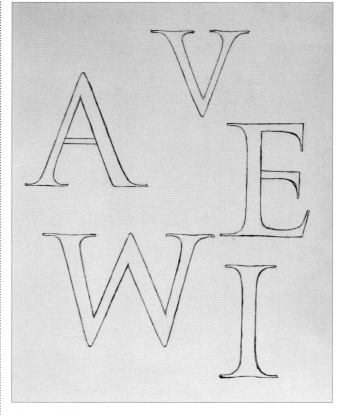

The original full-size line drawing

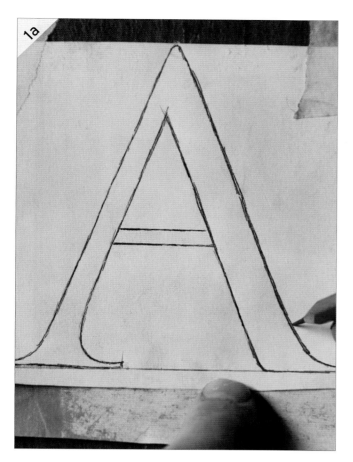

When correctly positioned, trace the letter onto the slate

Redraw over the faint traced line with renewed accuracy

SECURING THE STONE

Clamp the slate to the carving stand. Make sure the stone is secured safely and is held in the most comfortable position for you to work at.

TRANSFERRING THE DESIGN TO THE SLATE

Find the 'datum' on your piece of stone to take measurements from – the datum should be the straightest edge on the stone. If it is not straight or perpendicular, the letter will not look parallel to the ground. I used the left-hand edge of my slate. Draw a baseline for the letter and the horizontal lines of the 'A' using the white pencil/crayon and a tri-square.

1 Place the photocopied template or your own line drawing onto the slate and adjust its position by eye to balance it within the confines of the slab. Attach it with masking tape, insert the tracing paper and transfer the design onto the slate using a 6H pencil (**a**). Redraw over the traced image with the crayon or pencil, using the original image for reference. Make any necessary adjustments to the letter to be absolutely sure that the design works on the slate (**b**).

Tip Before you begin carving, designate a small practice area near the end of the piece of slate. This is not only useful for carving practice and familiarising yourself with the material, but also allows you to experiment with the type of finish that you want for the final carving.

Carefully develop the 'V' cut

Having chased out the centreline, start developing the letter

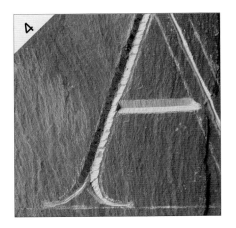

Use the chopping technique with care

Start to fine-tune the left oblique stroke of the letter

Developing the serifs

CARVING

2 Carve the horizontal part of the 'A' first. As it's the narrowest part of the letter, it requires careful development of the 'V' cut using the 10mm carving chisel. Carve it to an almost completed level of finish.

3 Starting at the end of the right-hand serif (as the letter faces you), chase out the centreline almost to the tip of the apex of the letter. You need to make a judgement here as to when to stop; just be aware of the vulnerable parts of the letter that need to be protected as you cut.

4 As you develop this line, try the chopping approach (see page 96) as this removes material very quickly. Take care that the edge of the letter does not become chipped with random pieces being accidentally removed. Look at the staggered chop marks and compare them with the finer horizontal carved section of the 'A' in step 4.

5 Using several passes and a steady rhythm, develop the 'V' until it is a similar standard of finish as the rest of the carving.

6 Start to develop the serifs at the left-side foot of the letter. A smaller letter-cutting chisel, such as a 6mm, may be better for this. Do not be tempted to just chop out at a triangle of stone; remember the structure of your brushed letters and how the serifs were formed. Develop the centrelines while retaining the flowing feel of the letter structure. Paint-filled brushes have a certain pleasing floppiness about them; try to reflect that in your carving.

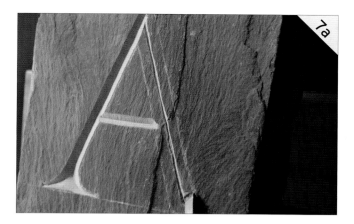

Chasing up the widest stroke

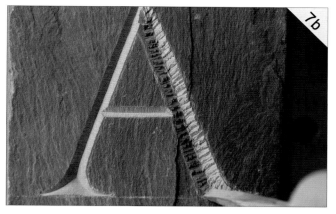

Quickly chopped out, with a margin of error

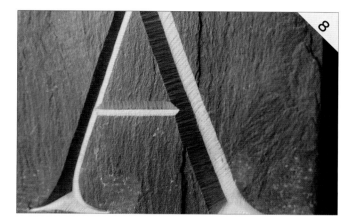

Notice the regular marks left by the tool

The finished carving

7 The last section of the 'A' is the widest part of the letter. It is influenced by the angle of the brush and the slight thickening at the bottom of the stroke as pressure is applied during the turning process. The stroke ends with a kind of flick as the brush comes off the page. Use the chopping approach again, but make sure you leave enough margin of error to keep well within the lines of the letter. Where this stroke passes the horizontal stroke the junction formed may be vulnerable to chipping and breakage; be aware of this but carve with confidence. (**a**), (**b**).

8 Finish off using the letter-cutting chisels to bring the letter to a similarly carved position for all the component parts (I have suggested three chisel sizes in the tools list above, but if necessary, you may complete all the work using only one). Due to the riven nature of the surface, different levels are present along the length of the carved letter. This often means that, when viewed head-on, the lines of the letter structure can appear to be slightly wobbly. Try to adjust this, keeping the tool at the same angle, although I personally would not get too hung up about it. If the overall effect is of a well-structured, pleasing letter then this should come across to the viewer. Slight, often perceived imperfections can add to the beauty of the letter but the end result is up to you.

9 Take a break, then come back to the letter with fresh eyes and the original drawing in hand and make a judgement as to how well the carving is working. Draw any adjustment lines you think are necessary, check your stroke widths and tidy up the letter to a finished state.

ROUTER TECHNIQUES

P UT IN its simplest terms, a router is a piece of machinery that quickly and accurately removes unwanted timber. Within woodworking industries, whole workshops can be geared up to mass-produce machined wooden objects with this versatile tool playing a major part. There are numerous cutting and shaping router bits and jigs for every imaginable routing project. There are also specially designed router tables, which enable large planks to be machined accurately with differing moulded shapes dependent upon the router bit used.

However, for our purposes I have focused on one machine, five straight cutters and one homemade jig. This cuts down on the expense and also allows you to focus on removing timber. Five cutters should be enough for tackling most of the projects you may wish to attempt. I have not used any 'V' shaped bits here as I prefer to cut these types of letters by hand.

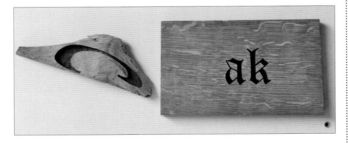

The completed pieces, routed, carved and painted

Routed Gothic letters, painted black to link with their pen-influenced origins

FREEHAND ROUTING

When we use tools such as chisels, pencils and brushes we are reliant upon our hand skills, combining hand to eye coordination in a relaxed manner with confidence in our accuracy. The same can also be said here in our freehand usage of this plunge router. Using the router in this mode, having stripped away all the unwanted paraphernalia, frees up the process, making the router just another tool to be used as a part of the creative process.

Freehand routing can be exhilarating, and removing the background from relief carvings or raised lettering quickly transports you into the working process. Razor-sharp tungsten carbide cutters leave a smooth finish that often does not require any or little further action. However, I treat this only as a roughing out stage, and will continue the carving using traditional methods and tools.

SAFETY

Many technical books have been written and courses have been run on the usage of this machine. Expertise of course takes time to acquire and safety is paramount. If you have never used a router before, please do not expect to be able to start the machine and instantly acquire satisfactory results. You will require training, not least of all to the dangers that this machine can pose if proper safety considerations are not taken into account and acted upon. If you are unable to control the router, any benefit in speed of action will quickly be negated by the need to repair a piece of work or a visit to the hospital!

Work on the 'Bench' project (see pages 170–77) requires the use of a router, but you will need a level of experience to enable you to rout out painted shapes of timber cleanly and accurately and, most of all, safely.

ROUTING EQUIPMENT

Woodworking or similar bench

¼in (6mm) router or similar – larger work might
require a ½in (15mm) router

A selection of router bits

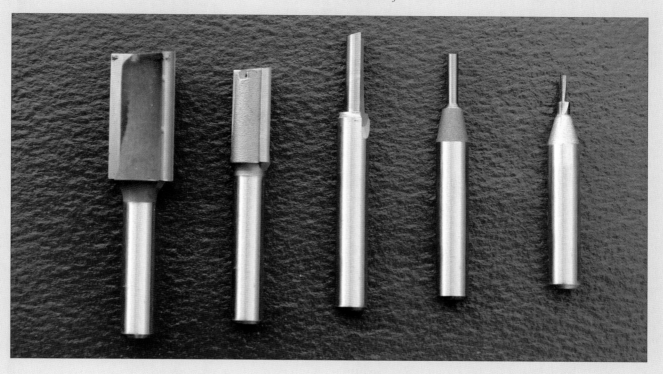

Cutters:

Two-flute straight ½in/15mm

Two-flute straight ³⁄₈in/10mm

Two-flute straight ¹³⁄₆₄in/5mm

One-flute straight ⅛in/3mm

One-flute straight ¹⁄₁₆in/1.5mm

Homemade 'wooden skis' plus manufacturer's parts;
for the router

Homemade wooden jigs to clamp the work to

TIMBER

Any suitable piece of scrap hardwood: I used a small
piece of riven beech (*Fagus sylvatica*) approximately
10in (L) x 3in (W) x 1in (D) at the highest point
(255mm x 75mm x 25mm)

ADDITIONAL TOOLS AND EQUIPMENT

6H/HB pencil

Stick of charcoal

Tracing paper

Chisel-ended paintbrushes: ³⁄₈in (10mm)
and ¼in (6mm)

Watercolour paint: red and black

G cramps

Pigment liner pen (0.1mm)

A small brush for dust removal

Glue

Screws and cordless screwdriver

Dust blower

Tri-square

Photocopier

Scissors

Health and safety equipment (see pages 46-7)

Demonstrating the plunge action with my thumb on the locking device

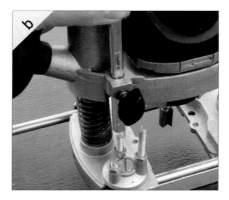

Setting the depth stop

Tightening the collet

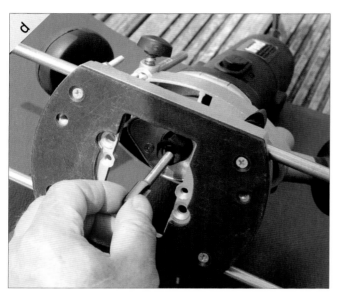

Insert the router bit in fully, then back off a fraction

The router on skis hovering above the undulating surface

FAMILIARISING YOURSELF WITH THE ROUTER

This particular machine is a variable speed spring-loaded plunge router, which can be locked into position. It has six speed settings for the revolving router bit, the minimum being 11,500 rpm and the maximum 32,000 rpm. As a general rule, the smaller the diameter of the cutting bit the higher the speed you can go. It has three interchangeable collets and I used the ¼in (6.35mm) (**a**). The depth of cut is set by a height adjuster and three-way turret depth stop (**b**).

Always switch the machine off and unplug it before changing the router bits. Then use the spanner provided with the machine to loosen the collet and remove the bit, while engaging the spindle lock (**c**). When inserting the new router bit, drop it all the way down until it touches the base of the collet, then back it off a fraction so it is not touching the base during use to stop the possibility of rubbing, damage and wear. Finally, tighten it into position (**d**).

Setting the depth of cut is very simple: stand the router directly onto the surface of the wood, or using the 'skis' jig, hover directly over the surface to be routed (**e**). With the machine switched off, gently plunge down until the tip of the cutter touches the wood, work out your depth of cut and adjust the depth stop accordingly.

Applying the skis

The work safely secured to a platform and the bench

Securing the work to the homemade platform jig

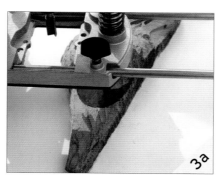

Check that all of the letter is accessible to the cutter

A smooth gliding action gives clean, accurate cuts

ROUTING METHODS

You are now ready to start routing using either of these two methods:

Method one Position the router above the piece of timber to be removed, then switch the machine on and plunge down using the router in a similar fashion to a pillar drill. Repeat this action with a slight lateral movement to the side of the previous hole produced to create a series of what look like drill holes in the timber.

Method two Switch the machine on and plunge down to a suitable depth of cut, then move the router between the outside pencil lines removing the painted negative space material between. You will have to do this in more than one pass to make a deeper cut. Never try to remove too much material in one go as this will slow down the motor and produce smoke.

SETTING UP THE ROUTER

1 Using parts provided by the manufacturer and some homemade wooden blocks, provide the router with two sets of 'skis' for differing heights.

2 Attach the pieces of scrap hardwood to a flat piece of smooth ply. This can then be screwed directly onto the bench or onto a homemade platform if you prefer (**a**), which in turn is then clamped to the bench (**b**).

3 Adjust the router while it is positioned over the pieces of wood so that you are able to access all parts of the letter/s (**a**), (**b**). By running up and down with the attached skis on this flat surface, the router is totally independent and unaffected by any anomalies that may be present in the surface of the wood.

Tip If smoke is produced during a shallow pass and you are not achieving a clean cut, your router bit either needs to be sharpened or replaced.

Using a fine pen to perfect the design

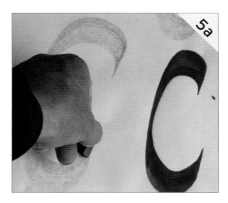

Several attempts with a charcoal stick

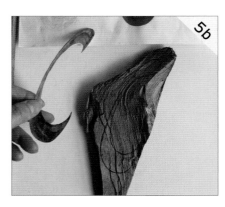

The chosen design, used as a template

Painting a letter makes it easier to see when routing

Carefully filling in the painted letter

THE DESIGN

4 In this example, I am using the letters 'A' and 'K' from the 'Oak Lodge' project. They have some very thin lines and a variety of other strokes to challenge your routing skills. If you wish to use other letters, please feel free to do so.

5 To complement the contrasting undulating and rough surface of the piece of beech, I added a hand-drawn single letter 'C'. This was produced with a stick of charcoal and a brush with watercolour paint (**a**). The design was photocopied, cut out and used as a template (**b**). The letter was then carefully drawn and painted directly onto the riven surface of the wood (**c**), (**d**).

Tip When hand carving letters, I generally start with the thinner letter strokes, especially where they join a thicker stroke at a junction. However, experience has taught me, particularly when starting a job, to rout out a thicker section while using a smaller router bit, thus giving a margin of safety and tolerance. I save the thinner sections for later, when I have familiarised myself with the machine and the way the wood is working.

106

The first part successfully removed

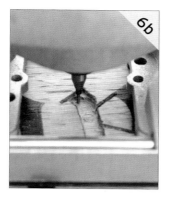

Edging into the corner of the letter

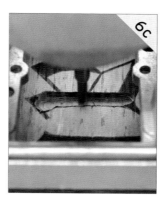

The second pass

Moving forwards to the next section

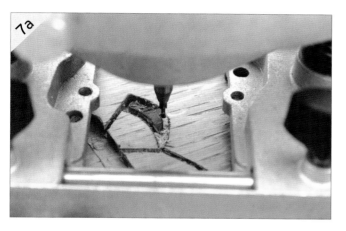

Drawing out the shape with a fine bit

An overview of the drawn-out shapes

Removing timber using the 5mm bit

Removing the remainder of the timber

MACHINING THE 'A' AND 'K'

6 You will need two bits for routing out these letters: the 5mm and the 1.5mm. Aim to make the strokes confidently and accurately in two passes. Starting with the down stroke of the 'A' using the plunge action and moving forwards, begin cutting using the 5mm bit (**a**). Then remove half of the remaining timber with the same bit (**b**), (**c**), (**d**).

7 The remainder of these larger strokes can be done using a slightly different approach. With the 1.5mm bit, draw round the letterform just inside of the outside line (**a**), with the results as shown (**b**). Then remove the remainder of the timber with this bit or the 5mm, whichever seems appropriate (**c**), (**d**).

Starting at the bottom and working upwards

The partially routed out letter

MACHINING THE 'C'

8 Using the largest bit possible, start with the thickest section of the letter and set the provisional base level. Change to the 5mm bit and proceed around the curve of the letter. Having plunged the router, without locking it into position, start at the end of the letter and work your way around, finishing at the centre of the thin stroke. As you gently move forwards, allow the router to naturally rise upwards, with the springs pushing it back up to its resting position. This should give you a smooth transitional cut from the deeper, wider part of the letter to the thinner, shallower centre part.

9 Once you have produced the desired cut, use the same technique starting from the other end of the letter and meeting in the middle at the top. This is not the only way to approach this particular lettering exercise, and care must be taken when routing from a deep part of a letter to the shallow part. Also, the timber you choose and the letter you decide to carve will dictate the way that you use the router. Safety is of course paramount, so don't take any risks.

Fully routed out

A high-quality razor sharp cutter can produce exceptional results

When fully routed out the shadow produced allows you to read the letterform

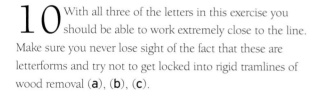

Fine-tuning the letter shape with chisels

10 With all three of the letters in this exercise you should be able to work extremely close to the line. Make sure you never lose sight of the fact that these are letterforms and try not to get locked into rigid tramlines of wood removal (**a**), (**b**), (**c**).

11 Make any minor adjustments to tweak the letters with the appropriate chisels.

12 Finally, if desired, paint the letters with watercolour paint to add an additional finish. This was a test piece never destined to be outside so I used the first available paint I found.

Tip If you start to experience problems with the plunging action of the machine this may well be due to wood dust clogging up the router mechanism. This dust should be removed immediately.

Painting the carved design

GILDING A LETTER

WHEN CONSIDERING the finishing stages for both wood and stone-carved projects, I tend to adhere to the well-used phrase, less is more. For wood carved projects, I generally just add oil to finish it. With stone I tend to leave it to weather naturally outside, although I have on occasion used a little wax to enhance certain types of stone, such as slate, for example. A lot depends upon the type of material you are using.

Sometimes of course it is good to try something different, particularly when enhancing the letter carving. Painting them is one way, but why not have a go at gilding them? This is a process whereby you add gold leaf or paint to the carving to produce a beautiful, opulent finish. Gilding can add gravitas to a project, should survive outside in all weathers and is also a continuation of the practice process. It can be applied to both wood- and stone-carved letters.

TOOLS AND EQUIPMENT

Yellow enamel paint

Paintbrushes, any standard sizes (I used a ¼in/6mm chisel-ended brush)

Gilding equipment: mop, knife, squirrel/synthetic tip, gilder's cushion

Gold size

Turpentine or white spirit, to clean brushes between processes

Masking tape

Gold leaf, loose or transfer

Scalpel

Beeswax

The gilding equipment

A carefully painted practice area

Differing carved levels used as gilding practice

Carefully painted horizontal stroke

1 I decided that the slate letter 'A' I'd carved as part of the stone carving techniques would benefit from gilding. To begin, carve some random shapes onto the slate, then paint and gild them to give an idea of the visual effect the finished letter might have (**a**), (**b**).

2 Use yellow enamel paint and a small chisel-ended paintbrush to paint the letter, starting with the cross-section of the letter 'A'. Take care not to spill over onto the front surface of the slate or form globules of paint at the bottom of the 'V' or the tails of the serifs. A couple of coats of paint will probably be necessary to get full and even coverage, but with-out any loss of detail of the carved surface.

Don't apply the paint too thickly

Apply an even coat of gold size

Get everything prepared before applying the gold size

3 Take extra care to preserve the shapes of the letterstrokes. It is not just a matter of filling in between the lines but is a continuation in your understanding of the letterform.

4 When the paint has fully dried, paint on the gold size with the same attention to detail as given in the painting process (**a**), (**b**). Remember that wherever this glue is applied, the gold leaf will stick.

Wait for the gold size to dry. To test it, gently touch it – if you leave your fingerprint behind, it is not yet ready, a very slight resistance is all you are looking for. The drying time will vary depending on brand used, the ambient temperature and weather conditions. The particular size I used had a three-hour suggested drying time but as it was a warm day, it was ready to use in about an hour and a half.

Cutting the gold leaf

Lift the gold leaf and float it into position onto the cushion so it is lying flat

Do not breathe next to the gold leaf or it will float away

Having prepared the tip, deftly pick up the gold leaf

5 Rest a gold leaf on the gilder's cushion and cut it into manageable sections using the gilder's knife. Your working environment should be draught free and try not to breathe directly onto the gold or it may float away (**a**), (**b**), (**c**).

Prepare the gilder's tip either by rubbing Vaseline onto your arm and flicking the tip over that area, or by running the tip through your hair a couple of times. Thus primed, the tip is then used to pick up the gold and gently transfer it onto the letter surface.

6 Picking up the gold leaf and transferring it onto the prepared surface takes a bit of practice. Hover the gilder's tip over the section of gold leaf and deftly pick it up; lightly transfer it over to the section of letter to be gilded. Do not be tempted to transfer a large section of leaf until you become highly skilled or you may end up in a bit of a muddle. The leaf should almost float across to where you place it decisively in the correct position. Do not try to move the leaf if it does not land exactly where you wanted it to – you only get one shot at it!

Pick up and apply as much gold leaf as is needed to cover the letter. You will, I am sure, have a lot of waste gold leaf if you are new to gilding, but don't let that put you off. Apply smaller and smaller pieces into the missed areas but again, do not fiddle. Deft precision is what you are aiming for.

Having applied as much gold leaf as possible, gently tap it with the end of the gilder's tip to aid contact with the gold size. If necessary, you can use a still soft but slightly stiffer brush to further firm things down.

Collect the finings

Brush away to expose the gilded surface

Fine-tune the shape of the letter

7 When you are satisfied that enough gold has been laid, use a brush known as a gilder's mop to gently brush away any waste gold that is not stuck to the size (**a**). Collect these finings into a suitable container for future use (**b**). With all this superfluous gold removed, examine the letter in good light checking for yellow painted sections that have not been gilded. If the size has not yet completely dried, it is just a matter of picking up the collected gold finings and applying them with the mop. If it is necessary to apply more gold size, use a very small paintbrush and carefully apply it only to those small missed areas. After the appropriate amount of time, reapply more gold leaf or finings to finish things off.

8 Use a scalpel to gently remove small pieces of gold to fine-tune the letter shape. Be careful not to overwork this process. If care has been taken in earlier stages it should not be necessary to spend very long on this.

Tip The 'V' cut profile can be difficult to gild. Try approaching it from both sides until you meet in the middle at the junction. If you try to cover both sides simultaneously at this bottom junction with a single piece of gold leaf, it may stretch over and not actually be in contact underneath. It is likely to be suspended above a gap, so when you tap it with the gilder's tip it will break and stick to either side leaving an uncovered section at the bottom.

Cleaning up the practice area

Notice how the chisel marks still show through even after the gilding is complete

9 Using a section next to the practice carvings as a test area, apply some beeswax to see how this works (**a**). If you are happy with this finish, wax the whole piece. This will re-move any scuff marks and gave a slightly darker and richer appearance, pulling everything together (**b**), (**c**).

The finished carving positioned next to the original drawing

·THE PROJECTS·

This section of the book can be used in a variety of ways.
You could copy the projects directly onto the wood or stone blank
using the templates I have drawn, or you could modify the projects,
focusing on specific areas that you wish to change and make your own.
Or you could just use these for inspiration and create your own designs
while referring to specific techniques that help you progress,
as outlined in the previous chapter.

OAK LODGE HOUSE SIGN

I WAS RECENTLY commissioned to carve a replacement house sign in oak using Gothic script. For a project like this, my approach is to look for lettering that is as close to the original as I can get and which has a quality that I can engage with. I took inspiration from a 14th-century church screen, which includes a painted Gothic black script. Rather than using a sketch, painting or photograph, I decided to source a similar looking font from the internet. The timber I used was a European oak (*Quercus robur*) blank, which was clean, shake free, well seasoned and stable.

LETTERING STYLE

The technique used in this project is incised lettering. It is influenced by pen strokes rather than the brush, so be aware of this when drawing or tracing. It is very easy to inadvertently develop misshapen letters so keep a check on the negative spaces and keep thinking about the stroke action of the pen. This project naturally evolved into three parts: the letter 'O', the letter 'L' and all the other letters grouped together.

TIMBER
European oak (*Quercus robur*) blank:
20³⁄₄in x 5¹⁄₂in x 1in (530mm x 140mm x 25mm)

CARVING TOOLS
'V' parting tools: D12/2, 12/8
Gouges: D5/12, 3/22, D5/8
Flat skew chisels: D1S/12, D1S/8
Dummy/mallet

ADDITIONAL EQUIPMENT AND MATERIALS
Reference image
A drawing board set at an angle of about 60°, or a multi-slope with light window attachment, or a light box
Squared graph paper
6H pencil
Lining or tracing paper
Straight rule
Oil or beeswax

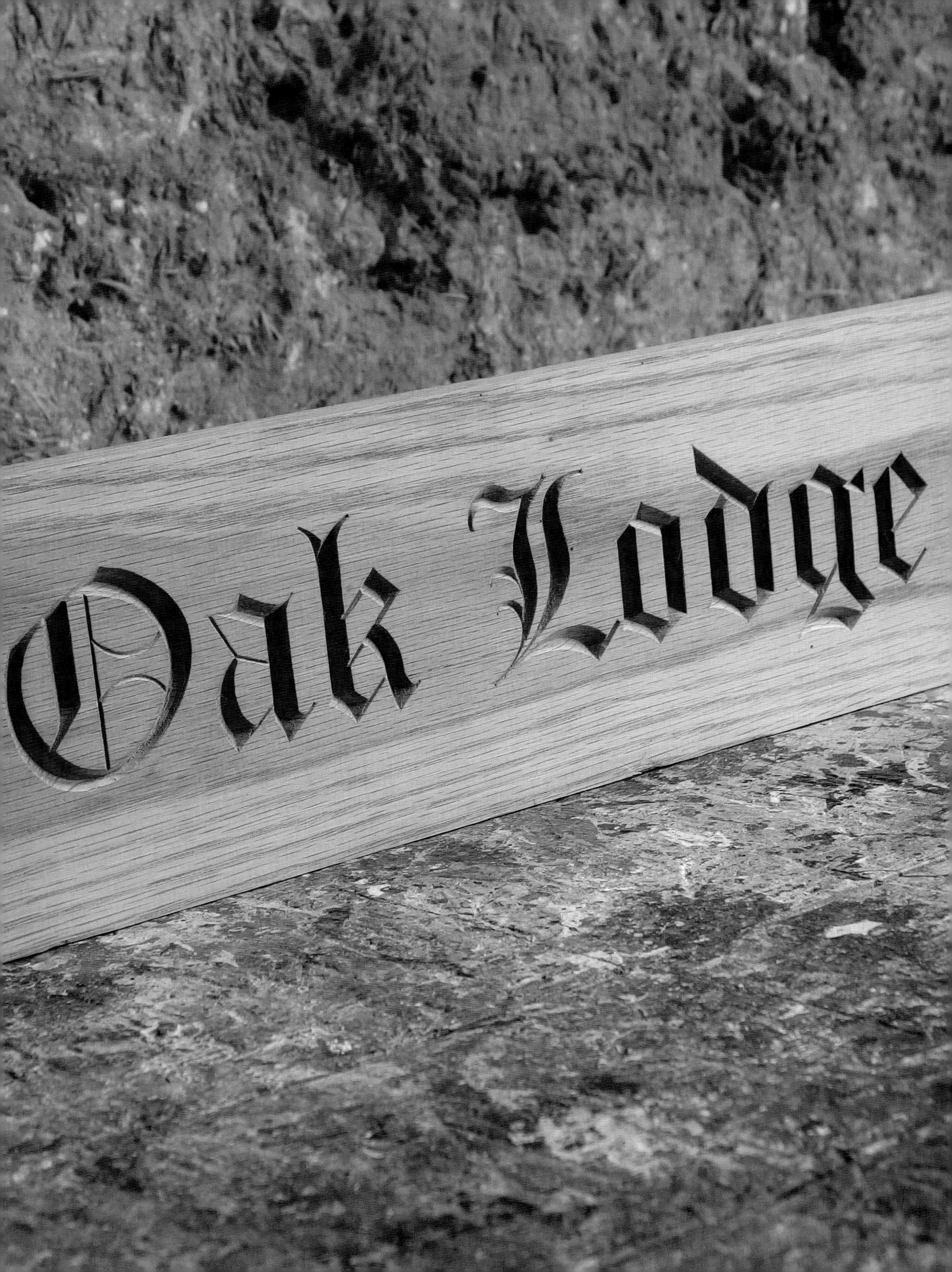
Oak Lodge

The 14th-century church screen that was the inspiration behind the lettering

Oak Lodge

'Old English'™ font

The hand-drawn template

The framed lettering

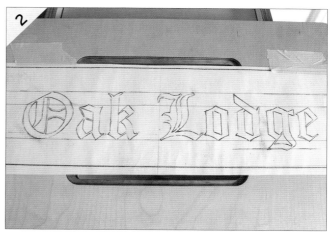

Lettering enlarged to full size

Making final adjustments

SOURCING, DRAWING AND TRACING

1 Download a font from the internet and print out the text. The font used in this project is Gothic 'Old English'™, sourced from MyFonts. Adjust your print to fit your multi-slope or light box. Draw a scaled-down pencil outline (I used 1:4) of the oak blank on a sheet of squared graph paper. Place this rectangular pencil outline over the image on the light window and position the lettering within it.

2 Trace this lettering, adjusting the positioning to get a pleasing visual spacing, then photocopy it up to full carving size.

3 Carefully trace this onto lining paper, making any further spacing or stroke width adjustments as required, while referring back to your original image of the lettering.

Tip If you wish to forgo the above three steps, you can use the hand-drawn template, left. Print a copy of this line drawing and take a careful tracing of it at the required carving size. You will note I have used a chisel-ended brush to fill in some of the letter strokes, and also highlighted a couple of the negative spaces.

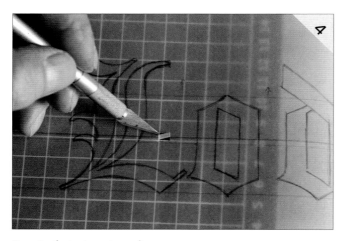

Preparing for tracing onto wood

Tracing using a 6H pencil

Carefully redrawing the lettering on the wood

Making a chisel cut from thin to thick

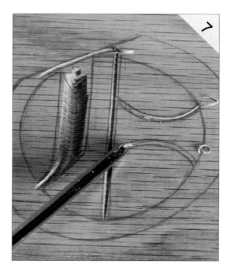

Chasing out the thin curves

TRANSFERRING THE DESIGN

4 Prepare your lettering for tracing on to the wood, including '+' points to help you with lining up (see page 69). Attach your oak blank to the multi-slope or your carving bench and draw on a pencil centreline. Position your tracing paper using the centre lines and '+' points as guides.

5 Trace your design using a 6H pencil (**a**). Then redraw over the resulting faint outline to darken the lines on your blank and, more importantly, to improve upon the design (**b**).

CARVING THE 'O'

6 You have several choices as to where to start the carving for this letter. My first choice was a chisel cut running from thin to thick with no need to worry about stop cuts as I was cutting across the grain of the wood. The oak was a pleasure to work and you will see that the cut was crisp and clean. You could also start anywhere within the circle halves, just make sure that you cut from thin to thick.

7 Next, you can start tackling the thinner areas of the letter. I was slightly ambitious in attempting to use the D12/8 chisel for the next stroke across the top of the letter, and decided to move down a few notches to the D12/2. This coped very well with the remaining thin strokes.

122

Starting the outside curves

Be careful with this cut; try not to run a split

Chopping down to continue the curve

Seamlessly joining the two curves together

8 It's best to make the vertical thin stroke first because it is a natural stop cut for both the thin semicircles that form the junctions. You can then move on to the curved strokes, but take care not to overwork these – at this stage, you just need to make a good start before working on them later with the curved gouges.

9 Now switch to the larger 'V' tool – the 12/8 – and work on the larger outside curves.

10 Having carefully opened up the 'V' cuts in these outer curves the remainder of the work, including the finishing, can be carried out using the 3/22 for most of the curve (**a**), and the D5/12 gouge for the base (**b**) with a few tweaks from the skew in difficult corners.

IMPROVISING A BULLNOSE CHISEL

Over the years I have collected upwards of 200 different shaped chisels, so for every job I can select a few favourites. I occasionally use modified tools – bullnose chisels – which would have been useful in this project when carving the 'O', but to keep your expenses down if you are just starting out, you can adapt standard chisels. To get the effect of a bullnose chisel, tip your curved gouges very slightly when tackling difficult curves and cut with care. You can thus avoid stabbing into the side wall of the letter. Having the corner of the tool in place also helps when going into a curved chip cut corner.

Chasing out the centrelines

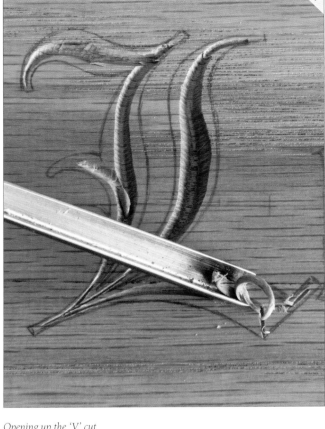

Opening up the 'V' cut

CARVING THE 'L'

The success of this letter hinges on the visual relationship between the centrelines flowing out from the leaf-type stem. During carving, bear in mind that the letterform needs to be balanced either side of a pleasing continuous line.

11 Use the D12/2 'V' tool and the mallet to quickly and confidently chase out the centrelines. With this 'V' tool in hand, you can now make a quick start on the other letters with thin strokes – the 'K', 'A', 'G' and 'E' – to save time later.

12 Now switch to the 12/8 and proceed to open up the 'V' cut on the 'L' (**a**). A lot of work can be done using the skew chisel (**b**), interspersed with applicable curved gouges when required.

Chopping with the skew chisel

Carving lines with the 'V' parting tool

Making a chip cut with the skew chisel

Chasing the top of the 'A' with the skew chisel

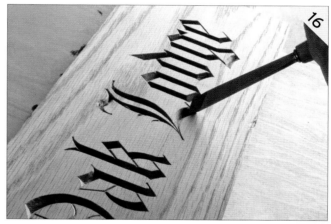

Chopping with the skew chisel

CARVING THE REMAINING LETTERS

13 As the remaining letters are similarly constructed using pen-influenced letterstrokes of uniform size, you can proceed quickly down the line, carving with the 12/8 'V' tool.

14 Use the skew chisel to carry out most of the remaining work, with help from other gouges as required.

15 Tackle the thin straight strokes present on several of the letters using the skew in a chopping down action, assisted by a straight rule if required. Take care not to make any contact with your chisel edge or the burr on your rule. Bring into play the full range of uses for the skew chisel (see page 82). If you have a firmer chisel or even a sharply honed carpenter's chisel in your workshop, use them for this task.

Tip The burr on the edge of good-quality straight rules can be used as a scraper in the finishing stages when you are working on large planks of wood.

FINISHING

16 Erase any superfluous lines or marks, giving a light sanding if necessary and then, using the natural light and shadow, carefully tweak the lettering until you are satisfied with the result. Try not to overwork it at this stage and keep referring back to the original printed lettering as a reference.

I decided to leave the wood in its natural state, but you could apply either oil or beeswax if desired.

ANNO DOMINI

THIS DESIGN was inspired by a 16th-century brass plaque. I was permitted to take a rubbing along with several photographs, for reference purposes and then made a limestone carving for use in a sculpture trail. For this book I decided to carve it again, but in wood, and at approximately four times the size of the original lettering on the plaque. I had two blanks of European oak (*Quercus robur*), which were clean with few knots and no shakes, well seasoned and stable. I used one blank for this project and the other for the first project, Oak Lodge (see page 118); keeping the timber pieces identically sized allowed a direct comparison between the brush-influenced lettering of this project and the Gothic pen-derived script of Oak Lodge.

LETTERING STYLE

The technique used in this project again is incised lettering. I decided that rather than focusing only on uniformity of stroke width and letter construction, I would add an artistic interpretation. I concentrated on the shapes of the negative spaces between the letters, particularly both letter 'N's, where they joined the other letters 'A' and 'I. The large tail of the letter 'A' balanced everything out, so I changed this slightly. I particularly liked the way the original maker had abbreviated the words by using a small letter 'O' and a symbol. Lots of these abbreviations can be found in this type of work, when they ran out of space or made a spelling mistake. They can be very pleasing and add life to the lettering.

TIMBER

European oak (*Quercus robur*) blank:
20³⁄₄in x 5¹⁄₂in x 1in (530mm x 140mm x 25mm)

CARVING TOOLS

'V' parting tool: 12/8
Gouges: D8/10, D5/12
Flat skew chisels: D1S/12, D1S/8
Dummy/mallet

ADDITIONAL EQUIPMENT AND MATERIALS

Reference image
A drawing board set at an angle of about 60°, or a multi-slope with light window attachment, or a light box
6H pencil
C300 detail paper (see page 34) or tracing paper
Wooden T-square
Straight rule
Oil or beeswax

The rubbing taken from the brass plaque

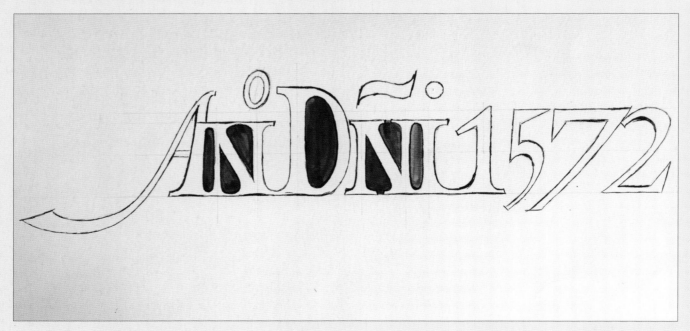

Template drawing

Squaring up the drawing

Adjusting the scaled-up drawing

The original plaque

Checking the spacing

DRAWING AND TRACING

1 Photocopy the template drawing and attach it to your drawing board or light box. Use the wooden T-square to square up the drawing and add top and bottom pencil lines. When satisfied, trace over this photocopy using the tracing paper.

2 If the scale of the template drawing doesn't suit your requirements use a photocopier to adjust it to the suitable dimensions, then trace the resized photocopy.

3 Alternatively, you could hand draw your own template drawing, while referring to the original plaque or an image of your choice. You can then put your own artistic interpretation into the design and gain valuable drawing practice at the same time. Whichever method you use though, trust your eyes and adjust the drawing as you feel is necessary – don't just slavishly trace over a design, always try and improve upon it.

4 Resolve any new positional and spacing issues that the photocopying may have introduced. Changing the position of the lining paper either left or right over the photocopied letters underneath while tracing will resolve the problems. It can look confusing when the letters don't line up; a solution is to insert a blank piece of paper under the tracing paper to give you a clear view of the newly drawn letters.

Transferring the lettering to the blank

The faint lines produced by tracing

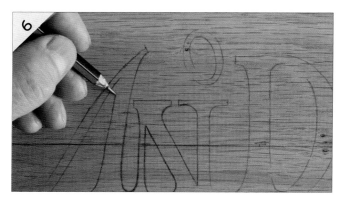

Drawing over the tracing

Using the square as a sighting guide

TRANSFERRING THE DESIGN

5 Securely attach the oak blank to the multi-slope or carving bench. Draw a horizontal centreline and place the line drawing into position. Remember to centre your lettering. The artistic licence in my own design meant altering the tail of the letter 'A' and the orientation of the 'O' above the first letter 'N'. I also adjusted the spacing to achieve the balance I wanted. When you are happy with your own lettering design, trace it onto the timber blank using tracing paper and a 6H pencil (**a**), (**b**).

6 As this produces only a very faint line, draw over this outline very carefully. At every stage, try to improve upon the drawing of the stage before.

7 Use a small tri-square to help you check that the uprights are correctly aligned. Don't be tempted to draw straight lines with it, though!

Drawing the letters upside down

8 This project is a design exercise as well a lettering one. The letters are very important, but you need to be aware of the negative spaces between them and of the beautiful shapes they form. This is an important aspect of interpreting and understanding all types of lettering forms. Drawing the letters upside down so as not to be influenced by their 'meaning' helps you to see the negative spaces.

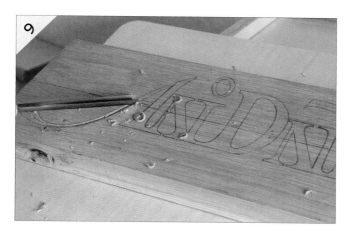

Using the mallet and 'V' tool to carve the 'A'

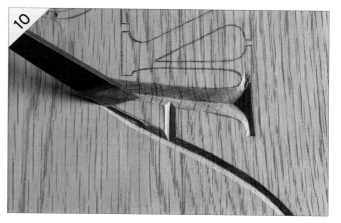

Take care with vulnerable short grain

The cross stroke and broad stroke of the 'A'

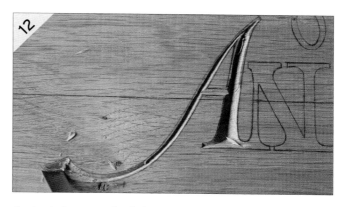

Carving the long arm end with the curved gouge

CARVING THE 'A'

9 Use the mallet and 'V' tool to quickly run up the broad stroke of the letter 'A'. My personal preference is to use a stone carver's dummy rather than a woodcarver's mallet. The first danger area is the bottom of the first curve, and in my case, this was exacerbated by a couple of knots. They proved to be no problem and I managed to carve the whole letter stroke in one continuous action using the 12/8 'V' tool without having to use a change of direction.

10 Using a continuous upward stroke means you should be able to avoid using a stop cut, which may cause splitting or breakages. Stop the stroke at the correct distance from the point of the letter and, with careful use of the skew chisels, you should avoid any problems with the vulnerable areas at the top of the letter.

Tip A continuous, uninterrupted stroke performed quickly helps with the look of the letter. It provides information as to how you, the tools and the timber are performing and is a confidence builder. If it starts off badly, do not be tempted to continue at the same pace. Take a slower, more considered approach: correcting errors made in haste is a time-consuming process.

11 Cut the cross stroke of the 'A' next and then start the broad stroke of the 'A' using the 'V' tool. Widen this strok, but avoid the vulnerable areas as discussed in woodcarving techniques (see pages 86–7).

12 Complete the end of the bottom of the serif on the broad stroke with a chip cut, using the curved gouge D5/8 in conjunction with the D1S/12 skew chisel. Carve another chip cut at the end of the long arm of the 'A' using the same technique.

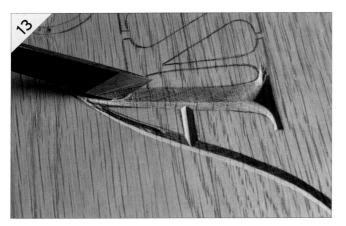

Finishing the 'A' with the skew chisel

Continuing with a curved gouge

Using the skew on the side of the 'D'

13 Finish the letter 'A' with a combination of the skew chisel and any other curved gouges you deem necessary. Don't be afraid to change direction if the grain warrants it; your oak will work differently to mine (see woodcarving techniques, page 78). Remember to use the light to check that you are cutting an accurate 'V' cut.

Tip Use lighting to check the quality of your work (see pages 48–9). A strong shadow and sidelight will highlight any anomalies, which can then be adjusted and re-carved. Any blemishes, unnoticed chisel cuts, badly drawn curves, inconsistent depths of cut or incorrect or inconsistent angle of cut will all be shown in minute detail. Also consider the lighting of the final location of your work and never stop looking at and checking your work as it progresses.

CARVING THE REMAINING LETTERS

14 Continue carving the remaining letters using the 'V' tools. As this project calls for a more 'instinctive approach' you don't need to complete each letter to a high standard before moving on to start the next. Try not to lose sight of the fact that the most important consideration is the nature and form of the letter being constructed. Link the combined serifs of the 'N' and 'D' with a singe stroke, using the D5/12. This should help bring your awareness back to the negative shapes between the letters.

15 Use the D1S/12 skew chisel to run up the side of the letter 'D' and tidy the letter. Strop the chisel to its sharpest edge before you do this as this gives a finish that, in my opinion, is unsurpassed by any other method.

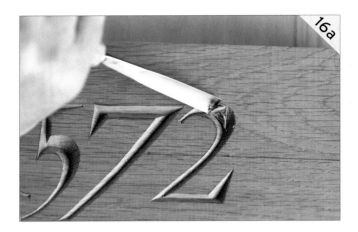

Paring down into the apex with a circular gouge

Finishing the curve

Cutting the '0'

Part of the completed carving in its natural state

16 To finish the curve of the '2', use the D5/12 curved gouge in two different positions, paring into the apex of the curve from the top (**a**), and then meeting at the apex from below (**b**).

17 To cut the '0', use the D8/10 and D5/12 gouges with the chop down technique shown in the woodcarving techniques section (see pages 78–88).

FINISHING

18 A light sanding will remove any grubby marks and pencil lines and will also highlight any further minor adjustments you may need to make. You can leave the wood untreated, or use Danish or tung oil to help preserve the work if it will be placed outdoors. Simple beeswax applied directly to timber can also give a nice finish.

ALTERNATIVE APPROACH

You may decide to take a formulaic approach to letter carving, using one chisel or gouge along the complete line of letters, then going back to the start to use the same procedure with the rest of the tools until the lettering is complete. This stabbing down approach can be faster but it can lead to the tool starting to dictate the shape of your carving. When carving calligraphic letters with numerous twists and curves I will use any and every tool I have available, cutting in whatever manner seems appropriate. Always try to ensure that the drawn letterform is not compromised or altered by the shape of your carving tools. When you consider the amount of time and effort already spent on your brushwork and drawing, changing the design halfway through a project doesn't make any sense.

BREADBOARD

I FOUND THIS Victorian breadboard a few years ago in a junk shop. At first glance, the impressive carving looks rather busy and there doesn't appear to be any logic to the design. Nothing though could be further from the truth. Rather than present you with a fully carved and functional breadboard, this will be a work in progress piece, partially carved. It contains original pencil lines that set out the positions of the different elements. I have changed a few things to make the work my own and these will be discussed as we progress through the project.

LETTERING STYLE

The board features raised lettering, which was based on a pen-influenced Gothic script. It is a quality carved piece which would have taken time to reproduce, while presumably being manufactured in large numbers to make its production worthwhile. It reminds me of the ethos of the Arts and Crafts movement, which rebelled against machine-made products, preferring instead to encourage skills, proper training and job satisfaction for the craftsmen involved. It even takes the moral high ground, incorporating the proverb 'waste not, want not'.

TIMBER

Circular turned beech blank (12½in/318mm diameter x 1in/25mm thick)

Profile shown can be given to a turner who can reproduce it onto the blank

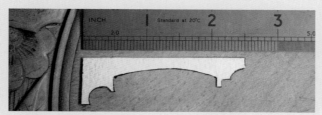

The profile used by the turner

CARVING TOOLS

Firmer chisel: D1/8

'V' parting tools: D12/2, 12/8

Gouges: D5/12, D5/8, D8/4, D8/10, D9/2, 3/22, 5F/8

Flat skew chisels: D1S/12, D1S/8

Veiner D11/1

Large 'off the flat', No. 1, 25mm dia.

Small carpenter's chisel, 5mm wide

Small forward bent tools

Dummy/mallet

COPYING A DESIGN

If you want to copy someone else's design you may well need to get permission. In the UK, copyright relating to artistic work (other things vary) lasts for seventy years after the death of the creator, or seventy years after the date of creation. However, you should always check the regulations before beginning a copy of a design. If you have the necessary permissions in place and access to the original, then there are several ways it can be copied. I was fortunate enough to own the original breadboard so I was simply able to make a rubbing for reference using a graphite stick. This valuable source of information was hanging on the wall in front of me as I worked on the carving. It also came in handy for the occasional calliper measurement when these were required.

A graphite rubbing taken of the original breadboard

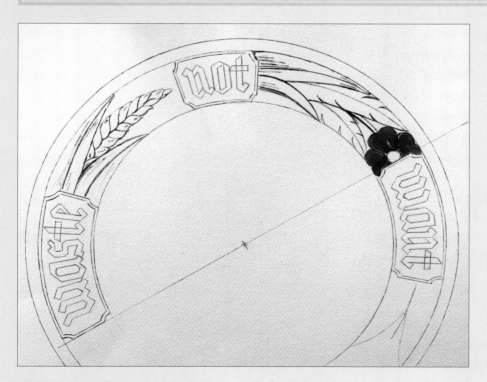

The line drawing with the modified lettering

DESIGN

Either reproduce the template drawing to a scale that suits you, draw your own version or source a similar breadboard and copy that. The original designer cut the work in half by repeating all of the elements of the carving. This means that you only need to draw half of the breadboard.

Trracing the design onto the turned blank

Carefully redrawing the design

TRANSFERRING THE DESIGN TO THE BEECH BLANK

1 Place the beech blank into the jig and mark the centreline. Then, using a rule, mark the positions of the carving elements. Use photocopies of the design to trace the two identical halves onto the blank.

2 Use a very fine pen to carefully draw the design on to the blank.

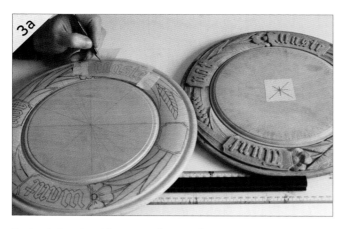

Tracing the lettering with an eye on the original

A comparison check between the drawings

See how the flower appears to be pushing upwards

Notice the space between the elements, different levels and parallel lines

The 'W' needed changing, I felt

ADDITIONAL EQUIPMENT AND MATERIALS

HB and 6H pencil
Tracing paper
Masking tape
Paper and graphite stick
Plasticine or modelling clay
Reference image
Multi-slope or workbench
Jig for multi-slope or workbench
Pigment liner pen (0.1mm)
A pair of compasses
Measuring callipers
Straight rule
Depth gauge or homemade version
Health and safety equipment

THE LETTERING

3 Trace the lettering onto the beech blank (**a**), (**b**). Even when copying a design, you can still adapt it to suit your personal taste. For my board, I decided to do my own thing as regards the design of the lettering. I understood the logic, for instance, of having a bar across the top of the 'W'. This reflects a Germanic-looking Gothic letter, and as a carving structure it was probably less vulnerable to pieces being broken off. Slightly ironic, perhaps, as one of the 'W's on the original board was damaged (**c**). It was not to my taste though, and similarly the 'S' I felt also needed changing (**d**), (**e**).

Carving the flower sets the scene for the letters

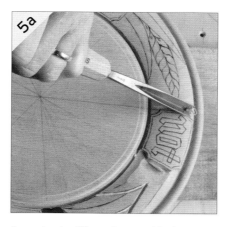

Separating the different elements of the design

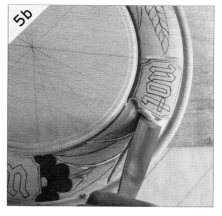

Quickly remove timber, but don't get carried away

The floral carving promotes the lettering

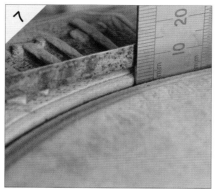

Measuring the level change from top to bottom

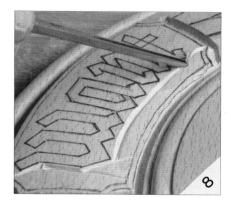

Setting in the lettering base level

CARVING

Fix the wooden blank firmly to the multi-slope or carving bench.

4 I won't go into detail about carving the floral elements of the design, however the junctions where they meet the lettering shields are very important. Carve one of the flowers and a wheat sheaf first, starting at the highest point and working down to the base level on the floral carving. Then reverse this when carving the lettering, starting at the base level and working your way back up.

5 Using the appropriate 'V' tools, separate the differing elements of foliage and shields while at the same time dropping the levels of the carving (**a**). Be bold at this stage and try to put yourself into the mindset of the original carver. Their carving, due to familiarity, was lively, done quickly but accurately. Using tools such as the large 'off the flat' 3/22 you can move things along quickly, (**b**). At this stage you might feel it a good idea to do some additional practice using scrap timber.

6 Carve the floral decoration, or at least the junctions of where it meets the lettering shields.

7 It's time to tackle the letter carving. On the original board, the turning of the blank produced grooves that separated the working part of the breadboard and the carved decoration. Using a depth gauge, find your base and top level measurement. The original measurement was approximately ¼in (6mm).

8 Decide on the height of your lettering and then, using the small 'V' tool, isolate the lettering by enclosing it in a box.

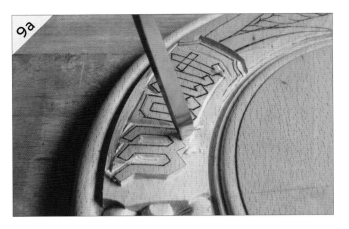

Letters are very vulnerable at the corners

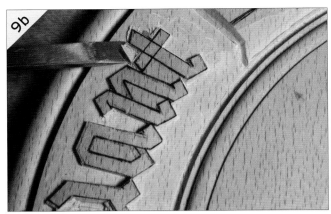

Carefully remove the chip without damaging the letter

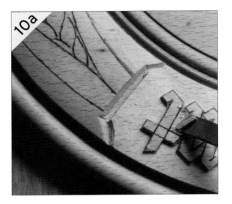

Don't bruise the adjacent letter edge with the chisel

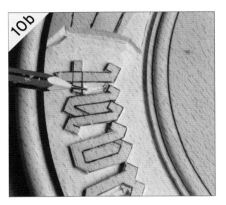

Adjusting the carving with a pencil

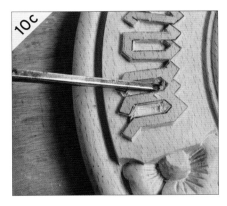

A small carpenter's chisel can finish off the cut

9 Using the small firmer chisel you can start to cut out the letters, while levelling the background at the same time. This is done with a combination of chopping down and then removing the section. One thing to be aware of is that as you move around the turned blank working on different parts of the carving, you will also be cutting in different directions, so the direction of the grain will be changing for you. If your tools are not razor-sharp or if you are slightly aggressive it is very easy to split off a piece of timber that was meant to stay. These letters are very vulnerable particularly at the corners if there are short grain issues, so it's worth taking some care (**a**), (**b**).

10 By angling the cut of the firmer chisel most of the timber between the letters can be removed (**a**). Take care that you don't go too deep or damage the wall of the adjacent letter. Use a small forward bent chisel or two to finish off the cut neatly, and keep a pencil handy to adjust the carving if things have gone awry (**b**). A small carpenter's chisel will also be very useful (**c**). Use the skew chisels to access those tricky inaccessible corners.

Tip When you are in full flow and concentrating on the carving it is very easy to lose sight of the design and the lettering forms. Take a step back, have a break and come back with fresh eyes. Always have the original drawing and other associated paraphernalia around to look at and reference occasionally. Always have a pencil handy to adjust the carving if things have gone slightly awry. Small design changes happen all the time; catching them early is always preferable.

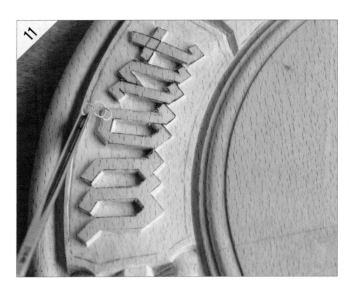

Deftly running along the edge, be confident

The piece completed to a point where all the different stages are visible

The piece seen from another angle

11 When the lettering is complete, add the borderline using the veiner.

12 Photographs (**a**) (**b**) show the breadboard completed to a stage I was happy with, showing all the different processes, from inception to completion of the carving.

STONE GRAPES

Throughout history artists and sculptors have used grapevines to decorate carvings and artworks. From a technical perspective, when carving grapes as a floral subject I believe they are hard to beat. Used as a guide the structure and nature of their broad leaves with the solid mass of grapes attached means the carving can be blocked out very quickly into strong solid forms. Then with additional work and clever undercutting, the carving is instantly recognisable from some distance. This project uses stone rather than wood, so the carving's longevity is assured if it is placed outside. I used a nearly square piece of Portland limestone, which had enough depth to allow high relief carving.

LETTERING STYLE

This is a high-relief carving, using a direct carving method. The style is much freer than that used in some of the other projects. The lettering does not have to be of a particular style or font but should develop naturally along with the drawings.

STONE
Portland limestone: 20in (H) x 12in (W) x 7in (D)
(510mm x 305mm x 180mm)

CARVING TOOLS
TCT straight-edge lettering chisels: 3mm, 6mm and 10mm. Use the 3mm for delicate carving; 6mm for tight corners. For middle sized areas, try to remove the maximum amount of stone with the 10mm chisel.
Carpenter's chisel/firmer chisel
Bouchard or bush hammer and dummy/mallet
Claw

ADDITIONAL EQUIPMENT AND MATERIALS
Reference image
Watercolour sketch pad or paper
Card
Watercolour paint
Blue spray paint
HB and 6HB pencils
Charcoal
Lifting equipment
Carving stand
Health and safety equipment
Chisel-ended paintbrush

The charcoal sketch

DESIGN

You will need to sketch out your design. The first thing to remember is to relax, be bold and remember these are working drawings, unlikely to grace a gallery. Keep everything you produce; diamonds often burst forth from dirt!

A valuable but rather messy working drawing

The completed line drawing

1 With my design, it became apparent that triangles were starting to appear all over the place, which linked the leaves, grapes and lettering nicely. I extended the penultimate drawing by adding another sheet of paper to create a large right-angled triangle encompassing every element of the design. Adding further lines wherever they looked right, I then placed the letters, wherever I felt they should go. This is an instinctive way of working that nevertheless uses all the skills you have learned.

Tip This can be a rather messy looking process and you may start to get lost. When this occurs I often place my sketches on a light box and redraw only the elements that I want to keep onto another sheet of paper.

2 Once you've achieved a design that you're happy with, you can produce a working line drawing. Because of the uneven texture and sloping nature of the stone I didn't want to tidy things up before sketching on the letters, and unnecessarily create work and lose valuable material. The idea of a stencil had come to me during the design stage and I decided to give it a try.

145

The first stage of making the template

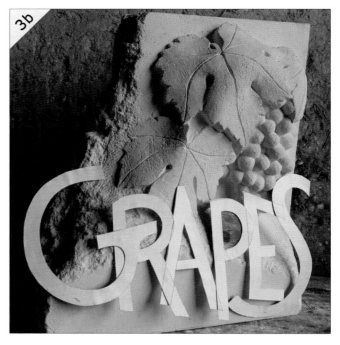

Positioning the template

Spray painting the design onto the stone

Equalising the stone

3 Take several photocopies of the line drawing so you can cut out all the different letters and glue them to a piece of card. (**a**). Having produced a working stencil, you can then attach it to the stone (**b**).

4 In a well-ventilated environment and following health and safety instructions, spray paint the stencil to transfer the design onto the stone (**a**). With this in place you can see how much stone will have to be removed to allow the formation of the letters 'G' and 'R' (**b**). This work can be quickly carried out exclusively using the claw.

After reinstating the 'G' and 'R' with a quick spray of paint onto the stencil, the task of releasing all the letters from the stone can now begin. Work over the whole design again, removing all of the blue negative spaces.

Starting to release the letters

Carefully removing a large chunk of negative space

The first cutover

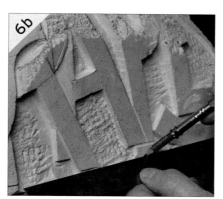

Fine-tuning the bottom of the letters

Adjusting the profile of the letter 'G'

CARVING

5 The first stage of the carving is to set in the lines of the letters using the largest 10mm letter-cutting chisel (**a**). Don't get carried away with the speed at which you can chop out the stone, try to be totally focused on the letterforms, the spacing considerations and the overall look of what you're starting to produce. Carve confidently with boldness and speed in a relaxed attitude (**b**).

Tip This carving is your own design and will evolve and change with each fresh decision that you make. Remember that a two-dimensional drawing will only take you so far, you are now working on a three-dimensional uneven surface. Try to get a feel for the shapes and undulations registering upwards from the point of contact the chisel has with the stone.

6 Block out the rest of the letters (**a**). This can be a good stage to take a break, then come back to the work later with fresh eyes. The textures on the stone produced by the different tools used are rather pleasing, so I decided that these tool marks would be represented in the finished work (**b**).

7 The letters 'G' and 'R' set the scene for the letter carving, curving gently around the end of the stone. Take particular care carving the curves of the 'G' where it crosses over the letter 'R'. Also, remember to look at the letters from different angles to make sure everything works.

Adjusting the centreline of the leaf

Marking the veins of the leaf

8 At the final stage of carving, carefully check the work for any anomalies and errors. You can use the flow and direction of the stems and veins of the leaves to further link the grapes and the lettering (**a**). Use a soft HB pencil (**b**), to draw the stems and veins in. The pencil marks will be removed in the final re-carving and finishing stage.

SEEK OTHER OPINIONS
Invite friends and family to give their honest opinions on your work as it progresses, because it is much easier to address problems at this stage. On my carving, several people felt the top of the 'R' and the 'A' needed additional finishing. I considered this to be a valid point and reworked the letters accordingly. I also overcut the veins so these were softened with the bouchard.

Now is the time to seek other opinions

Make adjustments based on the feedback

FINISHING

On my carving, I decided that parts of the letters would be smoothly finished, while other sections of the letters would not only show the residual chisel marks, but also some lightly worked marks left by the claw. Within the negative spaces of the letters I also left the original chopping out marks left by the claw. Using a large firmer, or old carpenter's chisel, carefully straighten all of the lines on the relevant letters.

When used carefully, a bouchard (or bush hammer) becomes a very useful shaping tool. It crumbles the stone away and leaves some wonderful marks. Take care not to get carried away when you use it – it is just to freshen things up and to incorporate some fine-tuning into the carving design. As a further contrast, use the large 10mm carving chisel to carefully finish off certain sections of the leaves. Again, don't overdo this; it is just adding some contrast in the texture of the leaves.

9 Finish the background area behind the grapes using a very fine wet and dry paper, then remove all dust from the carving. The right-hand crumbly edge of the stone was a natural feature which I liked, so I left this as it was.

BLOCK PRINT

AN EXHIBITION of chiaroscuro woodcuts produced during the Italian Renaissance was the inspiration for this project. During the 1500s artists such as Ugo da Carpi produced exquisite works more akin to paintings than prints. They were able to incorporate tones and highlights into their works by using a series of woodblocks to build up the layers. This enabled them to model figurative forms, for example by the application of more or less ink applied to the tonal blocks. They also experimented with colour to produce works displaying differing moods and intensities.

LETTERING STYLE

This woodcut design was produced using two blocks. Technically it should have been made using three but I decided to dispense with the third block to save time. With careful inking, the small red areas were incorporated into the second block instead. For this project structure of the letterforms is of secondary importance. I was more concerned with the letters being revealed due to the removal of simple but structured negative spaces.

TIMBER
Two tulipwood (*Dalbergia decipularis*) blocks: 7in (H) x 9in (W) x 1in (D) (180mm x 230mm x 25mm)

CARVING CHISELS
'V' parting tool: 17/6
Flat skew chisel: D1S/12
Gouges: D5/12, D8/10, D5/8, 3/22, 5F/8
Dummy/mallet

ADDITIONAL EQUIPMENT AND MATERIALS
Bench
Multi-slope or carving stand

Printing ink: black, red, blue
Printing or watercolour paper
Watercolour paints: black, red, blue
Chisel-ended paintbrushes: ³⁄₈in (10mm) and ¼in (6mm)
Paint rollers
Plate glass or Perspex
White tracing paper made using C300 detail paper (see page 34) with white chalk rubbed over one side
Drawing board and geometrical equipment
6H/HB pencils
Baren, wooden spoon or piece of timber, for burnishing
Pigment liner pen (0.5mm)
Photocopier

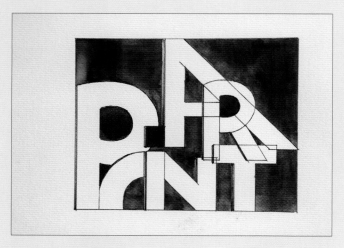

The chosen design

The key block

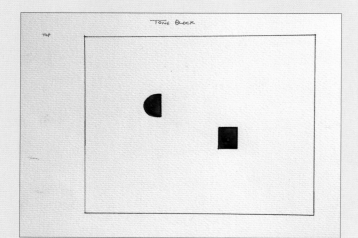

The background tone

The mid-tone

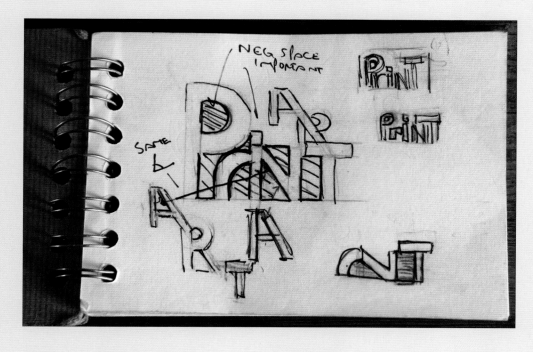

Sketching ideas and designs

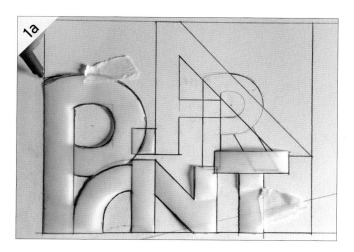

Using templates can help speed up the process

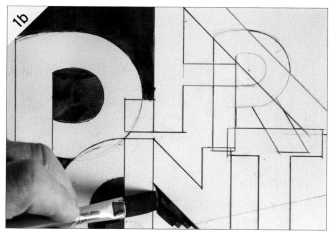

Carefully cutting in a tight corner with a brush

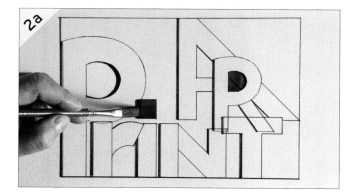

Working on another design, the second of three

Finishing off the third design with some careful brushstrokes

JIG

You need to purchase or make a framework that can be used to carve the blocks and to contain the block while printing. Each block needs to be in the same position for the print run so that everything lines up on the finished print. The frame should be lower than the height of the block residing in it so that during the printing process the paper only comes in contact with the printing block, not the frame.

DESIGN

1 Sketch out some ideas for your design. I chose the words 'print' and 'art'. I then painted two more versions of the design based on the same theme. To speed things up, I traced over parts of the original design with the pigment pen, and cut them into sections to cut-and-paste into the next two (**a**), (**b**).

A chisel-ended brush can be ideal for curves if angled correctly

2 Choose which design you want to print. I chose my original painting because it felt the most balanced and interesting out of the three designs (**a**), (**b**), (**c**).

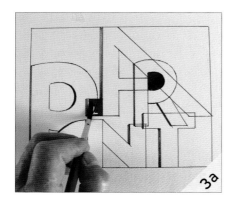

Adding in the design features for the third block, which in the end was not needed

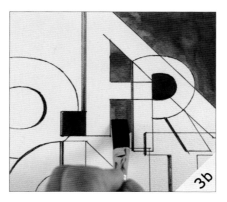

Carefully manoeuvring between the lines

Finishing off the chosen design

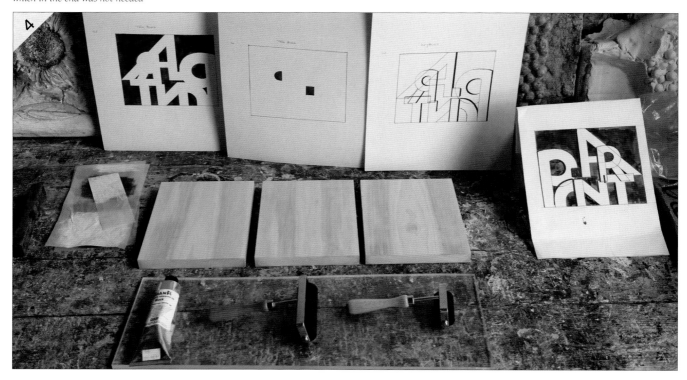

The printing equipment alongside the design material

3 Painting several versions of any design can be useful (**a**), (**b**), (**c**). It allowed me to experiment with colour and shapes, firming up ideas and helping with decision making. Design time is never wasted, particularly when things are not working out. I will often ask other people for their opinions and ideas, because once the carving starts any changes become costly in both time and money.

KEY BLOCK

4 The first stage of the printing process is to produce a reverse image of your design. I have produced reverse images for all three blocks (although I combined the red and blue stages to save time) which you can photocopy and use. Make sure that the image you use is of the same quality as the original drawing.

Tip While you're working on the reverse image, periodically check how things are working out by using a mirror to look at it the right way round.

Roller the ink onto Perspex or plate glass

Evenly distribute the ink onto the key block

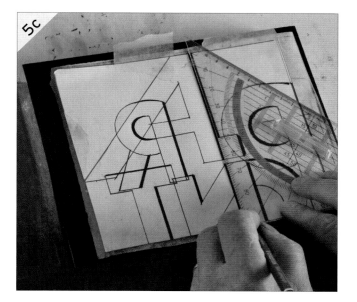

Tracing the reverse design onto the key block – accurate lines are needed

Cutting out the negative spaces between the chalk lines

5 Squeeze some black ink onto the Perspex or plate glass and distribute it using the roller (**a**). When an even consistency has been achieved, cover one of the wooden blocks with the black ink (**b**). When this is dry, position your homemade tracing paper under the design, with the chalk side face down. Use a pencil to go over the lines on the design to transfer it onto the key block (**c**).

6 If the chalk lines are very fine, you can use either a 'V' tool, skew chisel or a gouge to cut them and make sure they will survive the printing process. The angle of the tool and the angle of the cut allows you to produce a very thin top surface and a much thicker base. In cross-section, think of a pyramid with a flattened top.

Take care not to cut into the design lines

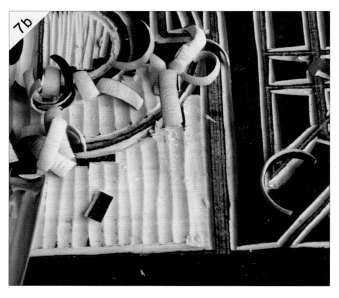

Having protected the lines, quickly gouge out the waste timber

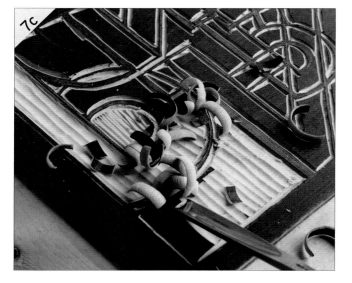

Gently shaping the curve with a gouge

Carefully ink the key block

7 Next, either chisel around the whole design with the D8/10 gouge, thus producing a protective barrier for the vulnerable lines, or chisel away all the waste material that is easily accessible and fine-tune the lines at the end (**a**). I often use a combination of both methods (**b**), (**c**).

Tip If your chisel slips and you remove a small piece of design line by mistake, insert and glue a tiny little wooden patch which can then be re-carved.

8 When you are satisfied with the results of your carving, your key block is complete. Use a roller to apply an even covering of black ink on the raised lines.

This first print is peeled off the block

It will be used to transfer the image onto other blocks

Carefully position the tone block in preparation, then transfer the image

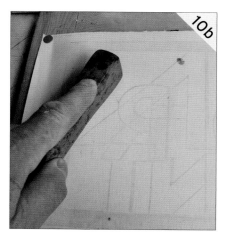

Transfer the design information onto the second block

A successful result ready for carving the next block

9 While the ink is still wet, pin a piece of clean paper to the frame surrounding the block. Firmly rub the burnishing tool over the paper to produce a print (**a**), (**b**) and peel it off the block.

TONE BLOCK

10 Place the next block of tulipwood into the same position in the jig (**a**). Place the key block print face down onto the wood and use the baren or stick to rub the image onto the wood (**b**). If you are using an additional tone block, you should still have enough ink on the paper print to produce the design onto that block of wood. It probably won't stretch to another one though so you may need another print (**c**).

Using the key block print, paint in the sections you wish to keep and use a pair of scissors to remove anything you don't want. Place this next to the carving to check that you are only removing the required areas.

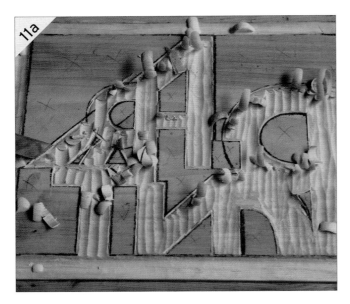

Tidy up the areas to be printed

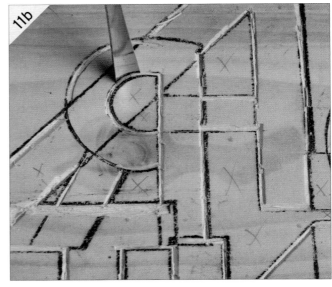

Carefully reshape the negative spaces

Gently sharpen the curve with a gouge

11 Make sure that the lines and angles produced at intersections are correct. A tri-square and geometrical equipment are useful for checking for inconsistencies. You can also use a skew chisel, gouge or a scalpel if required (**a**), (**b**), (**c**).

Occasionally check the carving against the 'cutout' print overlay

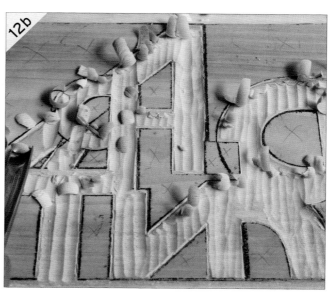

Remove enough material to produce the printing area

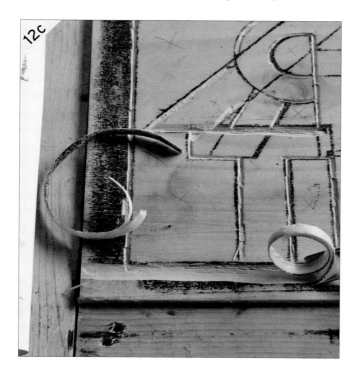

No stop cut was needed on this occasion

This type of timber was ideal for the printing process

12 Crispness of line is very important so it is worth spending extra time to get this right. The bulk of the carving can be done with the 'V' tool 17/6 and the D8/10 gouge. Additional tools can be used when required: for example, I used the D5/8 for the internal curve of the 'R' and the 3/22 for the external curve of the 'P' (**a**), (**b**), (**c**), (**d**).

This printing setup will now produce as many prints as you desire

A small homemade roller was used to apply the red ink

Apply evenly and take care to avoid the 'red ink' areas

Carefully position the paper onto the inked block

Burnish the paper while observing the reverse design painting

The first part of the process was successful

PRINTING

13 Use a clamp to secure the paper. Once the paper has been clamped, it is not removed for the whole of the printing process so that all of the blocks are printed onto it in the same position.

14 Carefully ink the blue sections of the block using a roller. Then avoiding the inked sections add the red ink using a smaller roller or a paintbrush if you wish. The end result should mean a fully covered and consistently textured block (**a**), (**b**).

15 Carefully position the paper onto the inked block (**a**) and, using the baren or other appropriate tool, burnish the surface until you can see the design embossed onto the paper (**b**). Refer to the reverse image 'design sketch' to help you visualise the areas to focus on during this process (**c**).

Tip I don't clean the blocks between printing and this can be quite useful when re-inking as there is a colour differential with the un-inked parts that can be easily seen.

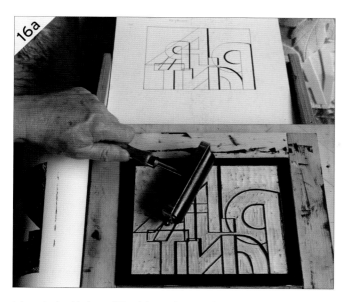

Inking the key block carefully while avoiding smudging the print

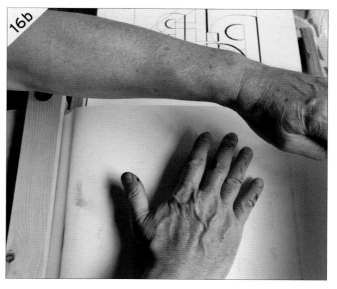

Carefully line up the printed paper and re-burnish

A successful print, with pleasing imperfections

The heavy-duty art paper adds the desired texture to the print

When you are happy that all the ink has been transferred, carefully lift the paper. Attaching a bulldog clip to an un-inked part of the paper will prevent it from springing back onto the block again. If you wish you can allow this to dry before proceeding to the next step, although you can move straight on.

16 Place the key block back into position in the jig, re-ink it (**a**), and again lay the paper carefully on top and re-burnish (**b**). The print is now complete (**c**), (**d**).

Tip Try using a variety of textured papers and different coloured inks. There are endless combinations you can use and the results can be very interesting.

STANDING STONE

THIS PROJECT, a standing stone, evolved when several serendipitous elements came together over a short period of time. First, this interesting piece of stone was rediscovered at the back of the garden, having lain hidden for several years, quietly blending into the background. Second, while chatting with a friend the subject of bold colours and churches entered the conversation, and I decided that the simple but beautiful inscription I had used before would be an appropriate subject with just a slight tweaking. So the standing stone became Anno Domini 2014 (in Roman numerals), using bright, colourful elements for the lettering.

LETTERING STYLE

There are several pathways this project could take, depending on personal taste and the qualities of the particular stone you use. I decided on 'V' cut incised lettering as I wanted to keep the natural surface of the stone as undisturbed as possible. It was a challenging surface to carve, full of pits and craters, hills and valleys, but I wanted to create a contrast between cleanly cut letters and the randomly chaotic surface of the stone.

STONE
A weathered boulder or stone suitable for carving. Mine was limestone with dimensions of roughly 20in (H) x 15in (W) x 15in (D) (510mm x 380mm x 380mm)

CARVING TOOLS
TCT straight edge lettering chisels: 3mm, 6mm, 10mm
Dummy/mallet

ADDITIONAL EQUIPMENT AND MATERIALS
Chisel-ended paintbrushes

Watercolour and white enamel paint
Signwriter's paint: red, blue, yellow
6H pencil
Hard white crayon
Paper
White tracing paper made using C300 detail paper
(see page 34) with white chalk rubbed over one side
Carving bench/stand suitable for supporting the stone
securely and at the correct height
Photocopier
Small brush for cleaning up

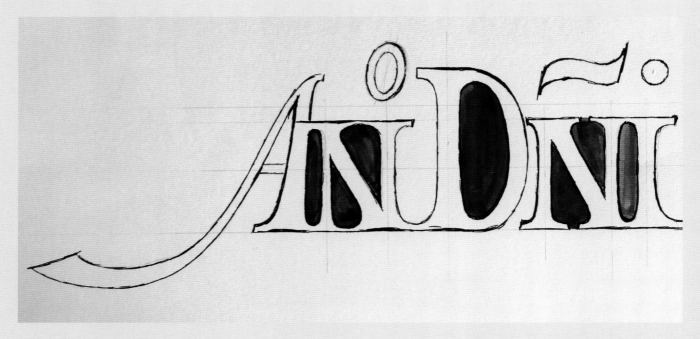

Template drawing

Numerals in Trajan font

MMXIV

Positioning the lettering by eye

Tracing through from the printed design

A fine line but visible enough to work from

Photocopy the Anno Domini drawing (left), scale it to size and trace it onto the piece of stone.

1 Cutting the drawing into manageable pieces and placing them into position on the stone is a quick and easy way to see how the final work may look when completed.

2 The paper used for this copy should be thin enough to enable you to trace through using the chalked paper underneath. The thinner the paper the better as long as it doesn't tear. The rough texture of the stone will make tracing difficult.

3 The resultant line drawing should be visible and accurate enough to enable you to carefully paint the design onto the surface using the chisel-ended brush. Remember you are shaping the letters, not just colouring in. You will need a delicate touch to capture that flowing form, and, as always, you should be aware of the negative spaces in your composition.

You need a delicate touch to capture that flowing form

Checking the positioning of the Roman numerals

DESIGN

4 The curves and shapes produced change when the brush is held in different orientations (**a**); experiment with this to tweak the letterforms. Trust in your judgement as to the positioning and size of the differing elements of the design rather than spending time measuring (**b**). Although rather crude, this speeds up the decision-making and draws you into the project.

5 The completed drawing or painting on the stone forms should give you a clearer picture as to how the final piece might look. More importantly, these initial stages are completely reversible if things don't turn out as you envisaged – everything can easily be washed off and you can start again.

The completed design on the stone

A tentative first cut

Carefully chopping out the stroke

The first roughed out letter

Tackle the other letters now

CARVING

6 Start with the flowing letter 'A' (**a**), (**b**), (**c**) and then work over the whole of the piece to move everything along at the same pace (**d**).

HEALTH AND SAFETY

You should take all health and safety issues seriously when making your own judgement as to the risks involved in working your piece of stone. I carved my stone outdoors and wore a dust mask and eye protection as I worked.

WATER DAMAGE

A few small pieces of stone flaked off as I carved. Upon examination, I noted that water had transgressed behind these sections and slowly delaminated them. There was staining consistent with this on the newly exposed surface of the stone. However, this was not a problem as I simply reinstated the missing part of the design and carried on carving.

Water damage causes some small pieces to flake off

A delicate brushstroke within the confines of the chalk line

Carving an unusual shape

After the final cutover

7 A carving such as this highlights the changes a design can go through as the project progresses, starting with the two-dimensional drawn or painted stage, then the applicaton of it onto the material to be worked, and finally the letter carving stage. The circle above the 'AN', which was drawn initially in a white chalk line, was totally changed with the application of the brushwork. I felt I wanted a more delicate line consistent with t he brush held in one orientation, thus it was further adjusted during the carving process. It is good to keep an open mind and have the confidence to change things if you consider it necessary.

8 Another cutover should bring you to the finishing stages and the final adjustments (**a**), (**b**).

9 Wash the stone, removing superfluous paint lines, chalk marks and stone dust. Draw over the work with a white crayon to prepare for the final cutover and fine-tune any elements of the lettering that you think need further work.

Washing down the stone before the final cutover

The final cutover, working backwards

Ignore the uneven surface

Sealing the larger letters

Carefully painting the letters

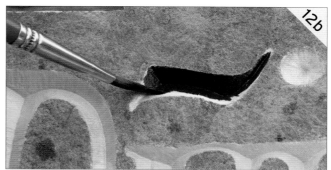

Use a smaller brush to finish off

10 Starting at the bottom of the stone, proceed with the finishing touches (**a**). Working from back to front, the theory is by the time you reach the beginning of the inscription you are carving, you should be producing the best work, which is of course the first to be seen and to be read (**b**). With the stone propped up on the edge of the bench, I was able to access the lower letters seated in a more comfortable position.

11 To enable the successful painting of these letters and to ensure their longevity when subject to climate variations, use professional outdoor sign writer's paint. Seal the carved surface of the letters with a white enamel coat of paint before applying the different colours. Any minor anomalies found in the letterforms can be corrected during this painting process.

12 The final arrangement of colour will be purely down to your own personal taste (**a**), (**b**) Once you've worked through this project, why not search around and source a suitable piece of stone, then use your own design and colour scheme to produce an original piece of work.

Project 7

BENCH

M Y INSPIRATION for the carving on this bench came from an impressive piece of stonework in a medieval abbey. It depicts a 'Marian' symbol, a monogram of the word 'Maria', dedicated to the virgin Mary. In the middle of the 16th century this particular example was installed incorrectly, either by accident or by design, so that the symbol reads back to front. On a simple slab bench I decided to add two carvings, one at each end. One of the symbols would be in the correct orientation, the other would be carved in reverse to mimic the stone carving. It was rather complicated so I decided to make a practice piece first to ensure the plan worked.

LETTERING STYLE

This project uses a variety of carving techniques to create raised lettering, with the background negative space removed by a router.

TIMBER
For the bench: seasoned European oak (*Quercus robur*): 48in x 10in (1220mm x 255mm)
The bench stands 18½in (470mm) high and the planks are 4in wide (100mm)
For the sample: European oak: 18½in x 10in x 1¼in (473mm x 255mm x 32mm)

CARVING CHISELS
Gouges: D8/10, D8/4, D5/12, D5/8, 3/22, 5F/8
Flat and skew chisels: D1S/12, D1S/8, D1/8
Carpenter's chisel
Forward bent tools
Dummy/mallet

ADDITIONAL EQUIPMENT AND MATERIALS
Reference image
¼in (6mm) router
Cutters:
Two-flute straight ½in/15mm
Two-flute straight ⅜in/10mm
Two-flute straight ¹³⁄₆₄in/5mm
Two-flute straight ⅛in/3mm
Small tri-squares: 90° and 45°
Pencil marking gauge
Depth gauge
HB pencil
Scalpel
Card/paper
For painting the sample:
¾in/10mm paintbrush
Watercolour paint

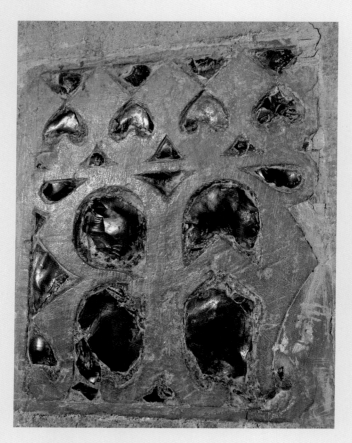

The original stonework

The Marian symbol in the correct orientation

The line drawing template (reverse orientation)

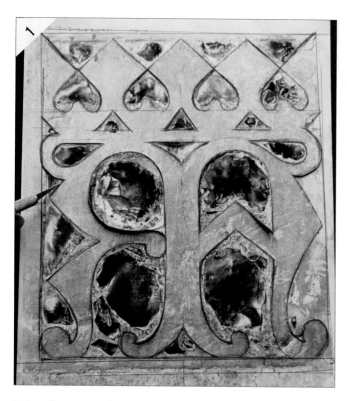

Making the paper template as a guide for the drawing

The sample piece placed in position

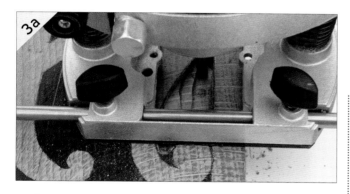

Gently using the router in shallow passes

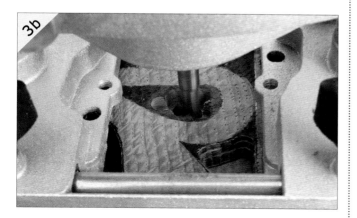

Demonstrating the plunge action of the router

TEMPLATE

1 Print a scaled full-size copy of your chosen symbol or use the template above. After redrawing over the design, carefully cut around it with a scalpel to make the reversible paper/card template needed to position the design on both ends of the bench.

MAKING A SAMPLE PIECE

2 To ensure the design works and for ease of handling, it's a good idea to make a sample piece first. Add the design to the piece of sample wood, then partially paint and partially carve the design. Take photos as you go to give you a record of all the different stages progressing from drawing to finish.

3 Using the techniques discussed in the routing section (see pages 102–109), rout out the negative spaces shown by the painted areas in the design (**a**), (**b**).

Carefully chopping out the design

A close-up of work in progress

4 Chop in to the carving using a combination of the curved gouges and straight-edged tools as necessary to follow the shapes (**a**), (**b**).

Tip Even when the bulk of the work is done with power tools the overriding consideration should still be shape and form of the design, so don't allow any of your tools to dictate this. When freehand routing you have to decide how much of a margin of error you will leave when approaching the drawn line. I tend to go as close as possible and either redesign or, if necessary, repair the errors rather than leave myself large areas of chopping out to be done by hand with chisels. You will of course make your own decisions, but take care not to ruin the work or compromise your own safety.

HOW TO REPAIR KNOT HOLES

There was a large knot hole in my bench and this had to be dealt with before I could proceed with the main carving. I cut a rectangular piece of oak on the bandsaw as a patch, drew around it and then routed out the offending section. I added a dab of wood glue, then clamped the patch in position and planed off the excess. In my experience, you normally get a better fit if you cut the patch first rather than trying to fit a piece of wood into an already removed section of timber (a) (b).

Checking the patch will fit

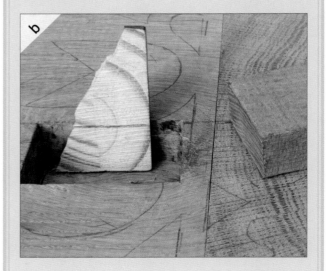

A simple depth measurement

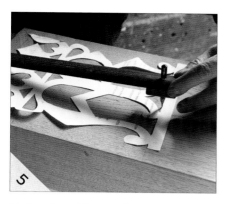

Marking the guidelines parallel to the bench edge

Using a 45° square to adjust the design

Carefully painting in the negative spaces

A homemade router jig

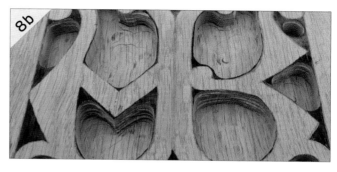

The shallow passes can be clearly seen

The base level is set by the homemade jig

BENCH CARVING

5 Fix the paper template to the bench in the most visually pleasing position. Use the pencil mark gauge to draw in the vertical and horizontal positional lines, one of which will be the centreline in the perpendicular plane.

6 Using the template as a guide, lightly draw the design on both ends of the bench, remembering to reverse it when changing ends. While referencing your original design, redraw the designs carefully on the bench by hand. Check your work frequently and revisit every angle to make sure that all of the lines flow nicely around the design.

7 As with the sample piece, colour in the negative spaces to make doubly sure that you don't make any routing errors.

8 Attach the bench safely to the routing jig (**a**), select the depth and remove all the necessary timber. You may need to make several passes before the required depth is reached, as is clearly shown in the photographs (**b**), (**c**). Note that no major burning marks are present. Such marks either point to a blunt router bit, or that the depth levels were set too deep for the router to handle.

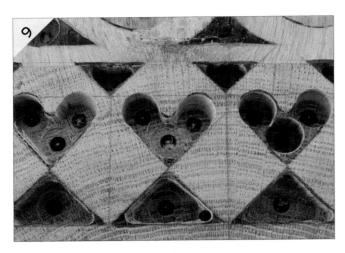

Three plunges, nearly all that is required

Beware the shavings don't obscure your view

Machining safely completed

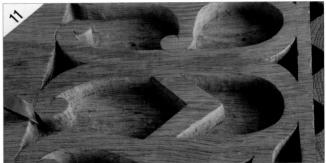

The final tweaking

9 The plunge action of the router was used to good effect when dealing with the heart-shaped sections in the design.

10 Photograph (**a**) shows the amount of shavings and dust produced in just one pass of the router, illustrating why the painted sections are needed to see the design (**b**). Even when used outside, all safety equipment should be operated in accordance with the manufacturer's instructions. (The plastic guard was removed for photographic purposes and this is not recommended by the author.)

11 Give the bench a light sanding then use all the available tools to give a final cut over to remove any wobbles and anomalies in the design.

FINISHING

12 Usually for an outside project you can just add oil, then try to avoid placing the bench directly on the earth so that damp doesn't chase up the legs. After being outside for a few years, the wood will turn a lovely silvery grey, no longer requiring much maintenance. However due to the changes it had been subject to, the timber decided to produce several small 'shakes' in the leg sections of the bench. So before finishing off the carving I decided to wait and allow things to settle and dry out a bit more. My bench now happily resides in the barn waiting for the day when I decide to finish it off.

WATER GILDING THE SAMPLE PIECE

Having a sample piece in this project allowed me to practice and compare the differing techniques and finishes, whilst experimenting with the colour arrangement and modifying the design. The sample become an attractive piece of work in its own right, and it also explained the different process to potential clients. This is particularly useful when creating and explaining large pieces of work which cannot be transported easily.

I decided to try out water gilding, which consists of applying gold leaf to layers of gesso and bole (a type of clay produced in varying colours including yellow and red). This involves a number of technical processes, and although you can pick up a lot of information from books and the internet you really need some professional help if you want to go down this route. The clay gives a flexible surface that means the gold leaf can be burnished to a very smooth effect.

NORNEY WOOD

I WAS ASKED to take on a lettering commission for a loggia which was part of a new build project – a timber-framed structure to be attached to an old property. The gardens were inspired by the work of the 19th-century garden designer Gertrude Jekyll, and located just a few miles from her family home. Jekyll was an acclaimed writer, so a quote of hers was chosen to adorn the loggia: 'the love of gardening is a seed once sown that never dies…'. The lettering to be used in the loggia needed to encompass three sides of the building, including its gable end. Using the dimensions provided it would be a large undertaking in terms of the material required and lettering size to fill the space – so it would be all about visual interpretation and guesswork in the early stages.

LETTERING STYLE

I was looking for a lettering that would fit both the period and ethos of the building and its location. One of the sources I used was a first edition copy of *Alphabets Old and New* by Lewis F. Day, published in 1902. The lettering chosen was by Patten Wilson, a British magazine and book illustrator. A lively font, it has the look of the Arts and Crafts period. The letters were sketched out to enable me to visualize them – and they seemed to dance across the page.

TIMBER
Three lengths of prime kiln-dried European oak (*Quercus robur*) with their associated phrases:

10ft 6in (L) x 11in (H) x 1⅝in (W) (3200mm x 275mm x 40mm) *The love of gardening*
9ft 7in (L) x 11in (H) x 1⅝in (W) (2900mm x 275mm x 40mm) *is a seed once sown*
13ft 6in (L) x 11in (H) x 1⅝in (W) (4100m x 275mm x 40mm) *that never dies...* Gertrude Jekyll

CARVING TOOLS
'V' parting tools: D12/2, 12/8, 12/10
Gouges: 3/22, D5/12, D8/10, D8/4, D5/18, 5F/8

Flat skew chisels: D1S/12
Dummy/mallet

ADDITIONAL EQUIPMENT AND MATERIALS
Reference image
Multi-slope with attachments or homemade supporting jig
Pencil marking gauge
C300 detail paper (see page 34) or tracing paper
6H and HB pencil
Tri squares, small and large
Photocopier
Modelling clay

A·B·C·D·
A·I·J·K·L
Q·R·S·T·
X·Y·Z.,,

E·F·G·H·I·J·K·L·
U·V·W·X·Y·Z. 12

E·F·G·
M·N·O·P·
U·V·W·
&. A B C D
M N O P Q R S T
3 4 5 6 7 8 9 0 .

A downloaded copy of the font Modern Capitals by Patten Wilson

Tip If you have several repeated letters in the text, take an additional tracing of the first completed one then use this as a template for the rest of the letters in the drawing.

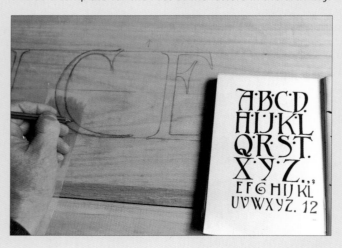

Getting the letters in proportion

The scaled-up lettering in position on-site

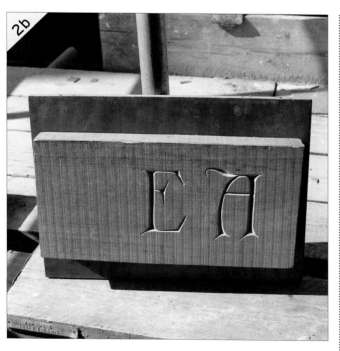

A sample piece can add three-dimensional impact

DESIGN

1 Write out the quotation on paper. When the letters all appear to be in proportion, take some measurements and decide what scale to use. I decided on a scale of 1:6. This meant that the finished carved letters would be between 5–6in high.

2 Use a photocopier or company that specialises in this work to scale up the letters so you can check them on site. A scale drawing can look very dramatic once positioned and allows the sample to be seen *in situ* (**a**). I decided to cut a couple of sample letters to help myself and the client visualise how the project might look when carved. These were full size and cut on a correctly proportioned piece of scrap wood. During the site visit and the installation of the scaled-up photocopies they added a useful three-dimensional aspect, particularly when placed at the correct height within the building space (**b**).

181

Positioning the photocopies onto the timber

Tracing the 'R'

Carefully redrawing the letters onto tracing paper

Marking out the centreline

DRAWING AND TRACING

3 Attach the photocopies to the oak planks as centrally as possible to verify that everything is in order. Then place a large sheet of C300 detail or tracing paper over the top of the photocopy and fix it in position (**a**). Use an HB pencil to carefully redraw all the letters (**b**), (**c**).

Tip When tracing over a greatly enlarged photocopy of a line drawing, remember that the original pencil line will itself be greatly increased in size and thickness. If you use a normal HB pencil your tracing may end up looking thinner and weaker then you intended. Work out your stroke widths before beginning the tracing to give you an idea of where to place your lines.

4 Place the first piece of wood on the stand and choose the edge that you feel is the straightest. Run your pencil-marking gauge down the plank producing an accurate centreline. Add the top and bottom lines for the lettering, making sure that the space below the bottom line is slightly larger than the top space, as this is more visually pleasing. Complete the work on every plank before moving onto the next stage.

Tip Even top-quality prime oak will not necessarily be perfectly straight. To check this, you can use builder's chalklines but you can also construct your own using a cheaply purchased line and two flints with natural holes in them to string the line through. This system was used to check that the lettering was straight and would be balanced over what was effectively a small arch over the whole length of these particularly long planks. I decided it was not necessary to straighten any of the edges, which would lose valuable width. I was able to adjust the drawing and carving so that this curvature was unnoticeable.

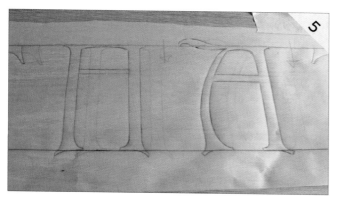

Adjusting the spacing, the arrows signify letting space in

Use this additional tracing when working on the other 'A's

Redrawing the letter

Continuing with the cutting

5 Attach your drawings to the planks, accurately lining up all of your pencil guidelines. Stand back and look at how it all works. Are there any spacing issues? Do the stroke widths need to be adjusted? Now is the time to eliminate any problems as later on it becomes more difficult. Trace your design onto the timber using the tracing paper. Adjust the letter spacing by moving the drawing one side or another.

6 Once you've completed all the tracing, redraw the whole inscription accurately, with the original font sample next to you to refer to. When the lettering is completed, position the wood where it can be seen in good light, stand back and examine it carefully. Ask a friend to inspect it too. It is important to then cross reference the wording on the planks against the original drawing. Check that there are no spelling mistakes or missing words. Redrawing at this stage may be painful but it is much worse to discover an error once the work has been completed.

THE CARVING STAGES

7 Making that first cut is always difficult but once you get started you will find that you will get into a rhythm. Much of the initial work will be done using the 'V' or parting tools, using the methods described in the woodcarving techniques section (see pages 78–88). It is usually best to finish a letter up to a reasonably high standard before moving onto the next. If the wood is cutting well, you may be able to tackle a whole word at a time (**a**), (**b**).

Tip If you want to check your angles of cut, turning your work upside down often gives you a different perspective. Perhaps you naturally cut more of a steeper angle on the left side of the 'V' than the right? Try warming a piece of modelling clay in your hand and then take an impression of the 'V' cut to check your angle of cut.

Continue the stroke into the curve at the top of the 'A'

Subtle, curved strokes continue into steeper curves

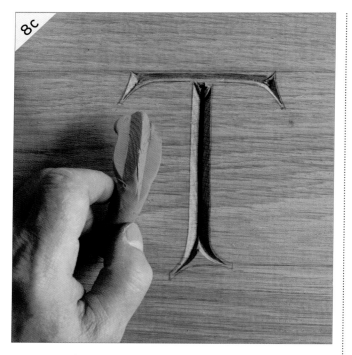

Using a piece of modelling clay to check the angle of cut (see Tip, page 183)

STRAIGHT LETTERS

8 It might be tempting to start using a straightedge or rule to draw the strokes in the straighter letters such as the 'L' 'T', 'W', the leg of the 'A' and the 'N'. You might be further tempted to use a large flat firmer or a carpenter's chisel to chop out the 'V' cut letter stroke. This way you could avoid the use of the 'V' tool and running up the stroke with a skew. However, a competently drawn letter will have a very subtle curve over the complete length of the stroke. In the long stroke of the 'T', for example, it is slightly concave, in parts of the 'N' slightly convex. Curved strokes often continue into steeper curves, finally ending seamlessly as serifs. I personally wouldn't try to produce these strokes using straight chisels. Refer to my methods shown in the woodcarving techniques section (see pages 78–88) (**a**), (**b**), and check the angle of cut (**c**).

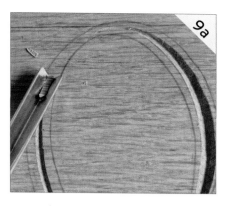

Starting the process of fixing the centreline

Tilting the 'V' tool; do not cut into the line

Take care not to run a split

Pulling the work together by adjusting the stroke widths, then a final cutover

LETTERS WITH CURVES

9 Remove as much of the timber as you can with the 'V' tool. For the 'O' for example, start cutting from thin to thick, with the top and bottom of the letter meeting in the widest section of the centre of the curves. For all of these letters, use a combination of the skew and all of the curved chisels to produce the pleasing curves that this lively font contains. Use the 'V' tool or the curved gouges to chop out the letter strokes. Try to avoid changing the letterform to suit your chisel shape. Do not lean back on the tool,

this can often bruise the edge of the letter (on a clean cut letter this can be very noticeable). Chopping down at too steep an angle can be another issue that is difficult to correct (**a**), (**b**), (**c**).

FINISHING

10 After lightly sanding the timber to remove any grubby marks, check the stroke widths and make any final tweaks with the chisels to pull it all together.

185

GLOSSARY

Ampersand A symbol derived from the Latin word, 'et', used as an abbreviation for the word 'and'.

Arts and Crafts movement A 19th-century/early 20th century movement driven by a need for craftsmanship, seen as a backlash against mechanisation.

Art Nouveau A style of art, achitecture and decorative arts (popular 1890–1914), characterised by sinuous outlines and natural forms, and particularly associated with Paris.

Ascender The part of a letter that extends above the top of the 'x'-height line.

Baren A circular shaped flat-bottomed tool used to burnish during the printmaking process.

Block print Prints produced by inking a series of carved blocks, which are then transferred in sequence onto paper.

Bouchard A double-ended hammer/mallet used for stone removal and shaping forms.

Blank A prepared piece of wood or stone, which can then be carved.

Burnish To firmly rub the back of a sheet of paper to pick up ink from a woodblock, using a burnishing tool such as a baren, wooden spoon or piece of timber.

Burr The raised edge on a chisel that is produced and then removed during the sharpening process.

Calligraphy The art of producing decorative script.

Candle The glinting light seen on the cutting edge of a partially sharpened chisel.

Cant The angle at which the writing implement is held in respect to the horizontal writing line.

Chisels and gouges Carving tools used in the production of carved letters.

Claw A multifaceted tool, producing 'V' shaped channels, used for stone removal and finishing.

Counter The internal space produced inside a letterform.

Delaminate Small shards of naturally formed stone layers which can flake off, generally due to environmental conditions.

Descender The part of a letter that extends below the lower x-height baseline.

Epigraphy The study of ancient writing and inscriptions found on durable materials such as stone.

Finishing The important final cutover of a piece of carving.

Font A particular size, weight and style of a typeface.

Gilding Decorative gold leaf applied to carved letters.

Horizontal stroke A letter stroke parallel with the x-height line, for example, the bar of the letter 'A'.

Incised lettering When letters are produced using a series of carving tools. 'V' cut is considered the favourite when letters are handcrafted.

Jig A device used to hold or support an awkwardly shaped piece of carving, sometimes used in conjunction with machining processes to help guide the tool operating on it.

Junction Where two or more letter strokes join.

Key block The first block produced from which prints are taken, then used to reproduce other blocks.

Letter spacing Either the measured or the visual spaces between each letter.

Loggia A room with open sides where one at least is facing the garden.

Mallet or dummy Handheld impact device used in conjunction with a chisel or gouge to carve wood or stone.

Majuscule Large letters that are either capital or uncial and all of the same height.

Marian symbol Lettering symbol referring to the virgin Mary.

Minuscule Lower case letters.

Modern Revival Refers to the influence of the father of modern writing, illuminating and lettering, Edward Johnston.

Negative space The spaces between letterforms or shapes. It helps to define the boundaries of positive space and brings balance to a composition.

Plaque A prepared tablet of wood or stone to which letter carving is applied.

Raised lettering Produced when background material is removed, leaving a letterformed shape.

Sample piece A test piece – a constructed element of a lettering design, often used to test design decisions in the intended location.

Scale drawing A resized two-dimensional drawing of a three-dimensional object or carving.

Scribe A person employed to produce documents before the invention of printing.

Seasoning timber The removal of water from timber, leading to a carving material that should be stable.

Serif A projection formed at the end of a brush- or pen-stroke constructed letter. Also used as a design consideration.

Shake Naturally occurring small splits in timber, produced during the drying process.

Short grain A term denoting vulnerable sections of timber produced when small carved areas are cut at right angles to the direction of the grain.

Stop cut A chisel cut used to stop a split occurring due to grain issues in wood.

Stroke width Designated measured parts of a letter stroke then used to provide continuity throughout the whole script.

Stroke sequence The order in which the letter is constructed, by brush, pen or carving.

Template or stencil A pattern produced in a durable material from a letter-designed line drawing, then used for the transferral of the image onto the carving material.

Vertical stroke A stroke at 90° with the 'x'-height line; for example, the stem of the letter 'R'.

'X' height The distance between the baseline of a line of type and tops of the main body of lower case letters; typically, the height of the letter 'x'. The 'x' height is a factor in typeface identification and readability. A typeface with a very large x-height relative to the total height of the font has shorter ascenders and descenders and thus less white space between lines of type. In a typeface with a small 'x' height, ascenders and descenders may become more noticeable.

BIBLIOGRAPHY

The Origin of the Serif
Edward M Catich
Catich Gallery, Saint Ambrose University, Iowa, USA (1991)
ISBN: 978-0-962-97401-4

Writing & Illuminating & Lettering
Edward Johnston
Nabu Press, Charleston, South Carolina, USA (2010)
ISBN: 978-1-173-37859-3

Just My Type
Simon Garfield
Profile Books, London (2011)
ISBN: 978-1-846-68302-2

The Art of Letter Carving in Stone
Tom Perkins
The Crowood Press, Ramsbury, UK (2007)
ISBN: 978-1-86126-879-2

Cursive Handwriting: Its History, Practice and Application
Philip A. Burgoyne
The Dryad Press, Leicester (1955)
(no ISBN available)

Carving Letters in Stone & Wood
Michael Harvey
The Bodley Head, London, UK (1987)
ISBN: 978-0-37031-019-0

Creative Lettering: Drawing & Design
Michael Harvey
Taplinger Publishing, New York, USA (1985)
ISBN 978-0-370-30613-1

Alphabets Old and New
Lewis F. Day
Kessinger Publishing, Whitefish, Montana, USA (2010)
ISBN: 978-1-162-58156-9

USEFUL WEBSITES

Woodcarving tools
Classic hand tools
www.classichandtools.co.uk
Tiranti
www.tiranti.co.uk

Stone carving tools
DK Holdings Ltd
www.dk-holdings.co.uk

Router tools
Trend
www.trend-uk.com

Artists' materials
Daler-Rowney
www.daler-rowney.com
Staedtler
www.staedtler.co.uk

Miscellaneous
Andrew Hibberd
www.andyhibberd.co.uk

The City and Guilds of London Art School
www.cityandguildsartschool.ac.uk

IMPERIAL–METRIC CONVERSION CHART

$5/64$in (2mm)	$2^5/8$in (65mm)	$8^1/2$in (215mm)	34in (865mm)
$1/8$in (3mm)	$2^3/4$in (70mm)	$8^3/4$in (220mm)	35in (890mm)
$5/32$in (4mm)	3in (75mm)	9in (230mm)	36in (915mm)
$1/4$in (6mm)	$3^1/8$in (80mm)	$9^1/4$in (235mm)	37in (940mm)
$9/32$in (7mm)	$3^1/4$in (85mm)	$9^1/2$in (240mm)	38in (965mm)
$5/16$in (8mm)	$3^1/2$in (90mm)	$9^3/4$in (250mm)	39in (990mm)
$11/32$in (9mm)	$3^2/3$in (93mm)	10in (255mm)	40in (1015mm)
$3/8$in (10mm)	$3^3/4$in (95mm)	$10^1/8$in (257mm)	41in (1040mm)
$7/16$in (11mm)	4in (100mm)	11in (280mm)	42in (1065mm)
$1/2$in (13mm)	$4^1/8$in (105mm)	12in (305mm)	43in (1090mm)
$9/16$in (15mm)	$4^1/4$in (107mm)	13in (330mm)	44in (1120mm)
$5/8$in (16mm)	$4^3/8$in (110mm)	14in (355mm)	45in (1145mm)
$11/16$in (17mm)	$4^1/2$in (115mm)	15in (380mm)	46in (1170mm)
$23/32$in (18mm)	$4^3/4$in (120mm)	16in (405mm)	47in (1195mm)
$3/4$in (20mm)	5in (125mm)	17in (430mm)	48in (1220mm)
$13/16$in (21mm)	$5^1/8$in (130mm)	18in (460mm)	49in (1245mm)
$7/8$in (22mm)	$5^1/4$in (135mm)	19in (485mm)	50in (1270mm)
$29/32$in (23mm)	$5^1/2$in (140mm)	20in (510mm)	51in (1295mm)
$15/16$in (24mm)	$5^3/4$in (145mm)	21in (535mm)	52in (1320mm)
1in (25mm)	6in (150mm)	22in (560mm)	53in (1345mm)
$1^1/8$in (30mm)	$6^1/8$in (155mm)	23in (585mm)	54in (1370mm)
$1^1/4$in (32mm)	$6^1/4$in (160mm)	24in (610mm)	55in (1395mm)
$1^3/8$in (35mm)	$6^1/2$in (165mm)	25in (635mm)	56in (1420mm)
$1^1/2$in (38mm)	$6^3/4$in (170mm)	26in (660mm)	57in (1450mm)
$1^5/8$in (40mm)	$6^7/8$in (178mm)	27in (685mm)	58in (1475mm)
$1^3/4$in (45mm)	7in (180mm)	28in (710mm)	59in (1500m)
2in (50mm)	$7^1/4$in (185mm)	29in (735mm)	60in (1525mm)
$2^1/8$in (52mm)	$7^1/2$in (190mm)	30in (760mm)	
$2^1/4$in (55mm)	$7^3/4$in (195mm)	31in (785mm)	
$2^3/8$in (60mm)	8in (200mm)	32in (815mm)	
$2^1/2$in (63mm)	$8^1/4$in (210mm)	33in (840mm)	

ABOUT THE AUTHOR

PICTURE CREDITS & ACKNOWLEDGEMENTS

Andrew Hibberd lives and works in Norfolk. He started carving at an early age and had a varied career before retraining as a professional woodcarver at the City and Guilds of London Art School. Since graduating in 2005, Andrew has established a successful business as a letter carver, producing original and restoration work for public and private commissions in wood and stone. He has written numerous articles on a variety of carving topics, is a regular contributor to *Wood Carving* magazine, and continues to find letter carving an exciting and absorbing subject. This is his first book for GMC.

This book is dedicated to Jane, academic oracle and patient wife. Also to David Holgate: mentor, friend and lunch partner, sadly missed.

Anthony Bailey/Mark Baker, GMC: pages 5, 118, 119, 126, 127, 134, 135, 142, 143, 150, 151, 162, 163, 170, 171, 178, 179, 192; page 10 (*The Rosetta Stone*) Hans Hillewaert; page 11 (*The Luttrell Psalter*) The British Library; page 11 (*The Seated Scribe*) Jose Ignacio Soto/Shutterstock.

GMC would like to thank Matthew Champion of The Norfolk Medieval Graffiti Society (www.medieval-graffiti.co.uk) for permission to use of all the images on page 58.

INDEX

Illustrated examples of individual letters are listed at the beginning of the relevant alphabet section, so, for example, any references to the letter A are found under the heading 'A (letterform)', etc.

To order a book, or to request a catalogue, contact:

GMC Publications Ltd
Castle Place, 166 High Street,
Lewes, East Sussex,
BN7 1XU
United Kingdom
Tel: +44 (0)1273 488005
www.gmcbooks.com